May ~~~~ ~~~ ~~~~~~~ ~~ ~~~~ surround you with love, peace, health, and abundance.

Blessings,

Laurie Hazel

Love Letters From The Angels

LAURIE HAZEL

BALBOA.PRESS

A DIVISION OF HAY HOUSE

Balboa Press books may be ordered through booksellers or by contacting:

Balboa Press
A Division of Hay House
1663 Liberty Drive
Bloomington, IN 47403
www.balboapress.com
1 (877) 407-4847

Print information available on the last page.

ISBN: 978-1-9822-4827-7 (sc)
ISBN: 978-1-9822-4825-3 (hc)
ISBN: 978-1-9822-4826-0 (e)

Library of Congress Control Number: 2020909544

Balboa Press rev. date: 06/09/2020

Dedication

With heart-filled gratitude to God, the Angelic Kingdom, my family, friends, and especially the Goddess Gals, whose inspiration and encouragement have brought these loving messages to the world.

Contents

Introduction

Several years ago, I began getting messages from the angels, encouraging me to write a book about angels and my experiences with the angelic kingdom. This book would be part of my life purpose and would bring the angel's messages to people in my own unique voice and format.

I called upon Archangels Michael and Gabriel, my guardian angels, and a collective group of angels, for messages and guidance for the book. *Love Letters From The Angels* messages were channeled and written down in a journal or were typed immediately on my word processing document on my computer. The channeled communication is written as the angels dictated them. Editing was done with the angel's permission on words or phrases that needed more clarification for the readers.

The book was created with forty-four themes or topics chosen by the angels. The number forty-four indicates that angels are among us and wish to connect with us. Nine themes are based on getting to know who the angels are and the roles angels can play in our lives. There are thirty-five themes that address ways readers can transform their lives with angelic inspiration and assistance.

Each theme contains a love letter directly communicated by the angels that speaks to each reader on a unique and personal level. We are all on a spiritual journey and the angelic communication will speak to us at the level we are in at that particular time and place on our journey.

The second part of the theme contains an Author's Note of real-life situations I have experienced and encountered with the assistance of the angels. The passages I have provided not only happened to me, but were guided by the angels to be included in this book.

The next section of each theme is called Action Steps. Action steps are crucial to an individual wanting to make loving changes to their spiritual, physical, and emotional life. The action steps are intended to be doable and easily accessible to most people. It is important to note that not all steps have to be taken. Readers are able to choose which steps fit into their lifestyle, capabilities, and comfort level. Some steps such as calling on the angels for guidance each day, should be done many times until it becomes a habit. Any step taken will bring wonderful changes to your life.

An affirmation is provided for each theme. Affirmations are positive statements that are loving messages for your spiritual, emotional, physical, and intellectual well-being. Affirmations work best if they are repeated throughout a day. It is also a good idea to post affirmations throughout your home or work, where you will see them often.

Prayer is talking and listening to God. Prayers are always heard and answered. There is a prayer suggestion for each theme. You are invited to use the prayer or use one of your own. Talking and listening to God each day will strengthen your faith, your love, and your life.

There is a journal page and reflection questions for each theme. When you take the time to journal your thoughts and experiences, the lessons will have a deeper meaning and understanding in your life. It is very rewarding to journal on a theme and then come back to it at a later time to reflect on how your journey has progressed. Each journal entry helps you discover who you really are and how valuable you are to our world.

This book can be read and utilized in different ways. One way is to read it cover to cover. Angelic messages vibrate positive energy and reading these messages will help you to vibrate positive energy as well. The second way to use this book is to refer to it when you are needing guidance and assistance on a particular topic. If you are going through some anxiety, then reading the theme on "Anxiety" will give you guidance and action steps to relieve your anxious feelings and help you become more peaceful. One of the best ways to enjoy and learn from this book is to ask the angels to guide you to the page you should read that day. Trust that the one you open is the one the angels have chosen for you to read. Angels use this form of communication often. Each time you read this book or a theme, you will learn new information or will have a better understanding of spiritual truths. When the student is ready the lessons appear.

The angels wish to be part of our struggles and triumphs we face every day. Their mission is to guide us and assist us on our spiritual path. It gives them great joy when we call upon them. The angels are messengers from God who help us to grow closer to God and each other. You are not meant to be alone in this world. God is always there for us every step of the way. He provides angels and people along our journey to help us discover how truly magnificent we are!

It is my passion and privilege to communicate with angels to bring this book to you. My prayer is that the messages in this book bring you great joy, happiness, and healing.

With love and blessings,
Laurie Hazel

Abundance

Dearest One,

The word abundance is often spoken of or heard in many ways by humans. Today, we would like to clarify what abundance means in the spiritual world. Abundance comes from God. God abundantly sends out his blessings to all the earth. There is no end to his abundance. That is the wonderful thing about abundance; there are no limits! The only limitations are those that humans put on the flow of abundance.

Abundance can take many forms. There is an abundant supply of love, money, time, and resources. All of these flow from God willingly to his children. Your job is to trust, believe, and accept the blessings God provides for you. Pray and talk to God about what you need. Do not limit yourself. For example, you pray that God will give you ten minutes for yourself during the day, without any outside interruptions. Instead, ask that God give you enough time for yourself during the day to renew, refresh, serve others, and to accomplish all the tasks required that day. God will give you more than ten minutes. He will see to it that not only do you have enough time but that you will have an abundance of time for work and play.

God will bring abundance to you in ways you cannot imagine. It may come through thoughts, money, people, or opportunities. Trust that God will supply you in the perfect way.

Lastly, we implore you to recognize the abundance God brings to you. Thank him for the gifts he has bestowed on you and that gratitude will increase the abundance in your life. This shift in abundance creates more abundance not only for you, but also those around you. The more you create, the greater the flow. It never stops expanding!

Love and heavenly blessings,
The Angelic Kingdom

Author Note

Abundance thinking was a big lesson for me to learn. I was taught by well-meaning adults and a strong religious upbringing to never ask for too much. Be happy with what you have. Asking for money is a sin. Having too much of anything is never a good thing. Those were deep-rooted beliefs that I needed to look at and unravel. I have always been better at giving than receiving. It has always made my heart sing to give gifts and to give to charities. I would give when I did not have the time or resources to give. I was often depleted financially and emotionally. One day, I got a message, "How can you give what you do not have?" That message hit me hard and stopped me in my tracks. It was reminding me that not only should I give to others; but that I needed to give to myself as well. It was a huge lesson and one I refer to often. I was going into debt and wasn't sure how I was going to get out of it. From that day on, I asked God to be my source of money, time, and love. Things in my life began to turn around. I had more money each month. I had more time in my day to spend on relaxation and fun. I was able to see new opportunities in my life that I hadn't seen before. I let God decide and provide what I needed instead of me trying to carry the load on my own. I always had asked for too little. Now I let God and the angels decide how big the abundance will be.

Action Steps

It is our thinking that limits our flow of abundance. I challenge you today to ask God for something that you truly want and need in your life. As you ask for it, stop and reflect. Are you limiting God in your request? Could you ask in a more abundant way? Call on the angels to help you ask in a more abundant way. Notice the miracles that come your way!

Affirmation

I am abundantly blessed in all ways

Prayer

Dear God, I ask that you fill my life, and the lives of those I love with abundance in all forms. I am truly grateful for your love and endless supply of blessings in my life. Thank you for your help. Amen

Journal Reflection

1. Reflect on and journal about abundance in your life. Are you in the flow of abundance or caught in lack mentality? Do you often express thoughts or phrases to others that keep you in lack or in prosperity?

2. Think about the feelings that invoke when you say or hear the following phrases:

> I don't have enough money.
> Wealth is for only the lucky.
> I barely have enough money to cover my bills.
> I will be in debt forever.
> There is no time for play.
> I work 24/7, and I prefer it that way.
> Playtime is for children, not for adults.
> I don't have time for a relationship.
> Love always seems to pass me.
> All my relationships have ended in disaster.

3. Think about the feelings that invoke when you say or hear the following phrases:

> Money flows to me easily and effortlessly.
> I am valued and my pay reflects my hard work.
> I am grateful for the money I receive each month.
> I have time for work, play, my family, and time for myself.
> I work hard and I deserve rest and relaxation.
> All work and no play is not the way!
> I am lovable and I deserve love.
> I am open to a new and loving relationship.

4. Starting today what can you do to bring abundance into your life?

5. A grateful heart recognizes the blessings God has bestowed and is open to more blessings. What are you grateful for?

Angelic Messengers

Dearest One,

We come to you today in hope that you hear us and heed our messages. We are happy to talk to you every day. We want you to clearly hear us. Our messages are important and vital to the world. Our messages will bring you peace, love, and joy. In fact, the word "angel" means messenger. We bring messages to each and every one. These divine messages are for you from God.

Our mission is to help you, protect you, guide you, and most of all love you. You play a vital role in our missions. Without you, we cannot accomplish our missions. Your role is to be open to hear our messages. Ask us to come into your life. God has given you the great gift of free will. We cannot and will not interfere without your consent. We stand by you, whispering guidance, loving you, and waiting for you to ask for our help in all matters. Nothing is too big or too small; all you have to do is ask. That is all. Simply requesting, "Angels" will call us to you instantly. Call on your guardian angels, the archangels, or any of us in the angelic kingdom, and we will answer your call. Think of us as your twenty-four hour hotline! You bring us great happiness when you call upon us. We are all too happy to help.

There are many legions of angels in the angelic realm. Archangels and guardian angels are the angels most called upon by humans. Archangels are powerful beings that oversee guardian angels. Archangels have no limit of time or space and can help many people at the same time. Archangels bring God's love, messages, miracles, and peace to all people who call upon them. Guardian angels are angels that are assigned to each individual person from birth until death. Guardian angels guide and protect humans on their spiritual and physical paths. Guardian angels never leave a person's side and their love is unconditional.

God wants all his children to enjoy life and the abundance of gifts he bestows upon them. You are God's child and you deserve these gifts and messages! Every person deserves help from God and the angels. It does not matter what faith, gender, race, or creed. All people are children of God and he wishes the best for all his children. It does not matter if you do or do not belong to a religious group or church. It does not matter if you have made mistakes in the past. These messages are for all people and will be interpreted differently for each individual's needs and spiritual path. We encourage you to journal, meditate, and act upon our messages daily. Call on your guardian angels, the archangels, and the heavenly kingdom to assist you in all ways and notice the beautiful life that opens up for you!

Love and heavenly blessings,
The Angelic Kingdom

Author Note

I have always been intrigued by angels, but did not really know much about them and did not hear much about them growing up. I knew that I had a guardian angel and that he or she would protect me. On my childhood bedroom wall, was a light switch plate with an angel watching over two children. I took comfort in looking at it every night. Then in the early nineties, there seemed to be angel figurines or angel plaques showing up in many stores. A friend bought me two angel figurines. I immediately loved them and my curiosity about angels began to grow. I noticed more people talking about angels. I saw a TV show about angels, and I read books about them. What I heard was always the same. Angels were divine beings sent by God to help us in all ways. Call on them in times of trouble and in times of joy. I began to call on my guardian angels to help me throughout the day and my life has never been the same.

Action Steps

When you first wake up, spend a few minutes praying and talking to God. Call on the angels to help you throughout the day. Before you go to sleep, reflect on your day. How did your day go? Did the day seem to go smoothly compared to previous days when you did not call upon the angels? If a problem arose, did you call on the angels for help? Remember, that this takes practice. Ask for help at least once a day.

Notice the difference it makes in your life. You may want to journal about the changes you are noticing.

Affirmation

I am loved, guided, and protected by God and the angels at all times.

Prayer

Dear God, I call on you today. I ask that you stand by my side. I ask that you guide me and protect me throughout the day and night. I am thankful for your love and assistance. Amen

Journal Reflection

1. Spend time reflecting and journaling on your personal knowledge or understanding of angels and the angelic kingdom.

2. Do you believe in angels? Have you had any encounters with angels?

3. Spend some time asking your guardian angels for help or guidance on an issue you are facing right now.

4. Begin asking for help and guidance each day. After a week or two, journal on how your life has changed since you began to speak to the angelic kingdom.

Angelic White and Pink Light

Dearest One,

Angels are pure light and high vibrational energy. The lights around us also correspond to the gifts we bring to people and your world. We are pictured many times as pure white light. Our angelic white light is all around you. It is brighter and more powerful than you can even imagine. It protects you, guides you, and surrounds you with eternal love. We ask you to take a few moments today and feel our love and light. Close your eyes and imagine white light pouring through you from your head to your toes. Notice how you feel. Do you feel loved and protected? Does your body relax and feel at peace? We truly wish you to feel love and peacefulness day in and day out. You may, at times, see flashes of white light or sparkles of light. When this happens, we are nearby. White light dispels all darkness, and nothing can ever diminish our light.

Pink light is the light of love in all forms. The power of pink light can attract new love and romance and heal broken hearts. Pink light can dissolve anger, bitterness, and misunderstandings. This beautiful light can remove obstacles and make a clear path for those who believe in this loving power. Pink light can bring love and harmony to war- torn countries or help an individual who has lost hope and needs love and warmth. Pink light is pure love, and love is the most potent force in the universe. When humans recognize pink light and love in all situations, they can begin to heal the world, their communities, their families, and themselves. Ask the angels to help you use this universal pink light to improve and attract only loving situations in your life and the world. Watch miracles happen!

Love and heavenly blessings,
The Angelic Kingdom

Author Note

I am a firm believer in the power of the angel's white and pink light. I can feel the energy and love it brings. I ask the angels to send white and pink light out before my day and to surround me with their beautiful light. When I do, my day goes smoothly, and everything falls into place. I know that the angels are working on my behalf, taking obstacles out of my way, clearing my path, and bringing more love into the world. If I forget to ask, I feel like little things annoy me. or it takes longer to accomplish tasks. It is something I do daily and is part of my routine. It only takes a few minutes, but it reaps great benefits.

When I taught first graders, we would ask the angels to surround us with white and pink light. If we forgot to ask the angels, my students could tell the difference in our day, our moods, or in our learning. The day didn't seem to go as well.

I also spend time asking the angels to surround other people who need pink and white light. I picture pink and white light around them. It is truly sending them love and light.

I recommend clients to ask the angels to surround themselves with white and pink light. Many have told me amazing and beautiful stories of how the white and pink light has helped them and their families. One client reported sending pink light to her children, who were estranged from each other. Another client used pink light to heal a work- related issue. Both circumstances healed in miraculous ways.

I also like to imagine the pink light surrounding our country and other countries. I picture angels at all four corners of a country. I picture the angels pulling a cover of pink light across the country. It only takes a few minutes to do this, but it is extremely powerful. The angels have told me that this simple gesture has done more than I can ever imagine.

Action Steps

Ask the angels to surround you with white and pink light and to send their light ahead of your day. Send pink light to friends and family members. Send pink light to those hurting around the world. Your actions, along with the angels, will create loving miracles that do and will change lives.

Affirmation

I am surrounded by angelic light. I am happy, healed, and whole.

Prayer

Dear God, I ask that you surround my loved ones and myself, with your beautiful pink light of love. I thank you for your love and the blessings it brings. I ask that I may be a beacon of this love as I pass it on to those who are in need of love and light. Amen

Journal Reflection

I encourage you to ask that pink light go ahead of your day. Take some time to reflect on how well your day went. It would be a good idea to journal about your day. How did your day go? Were obstacles eliminated from your path? Were you able to accomplish many tasks in a day? How did your relationships with others change?

Anxiety

Dearest One,

It seems like more and more people are feeling anxiety on a daily basis. It is normal for humans to feel anxious from time to time. However, if you are feeling anxious daily or several times a week, it is time to stop and check-in with yourself. What is causing your anxiety? Do you know? Is it interfering with your job? Is it interfering with your personal life? Do you have things to do but are so overwhelmed that you cannot finish any task?

First and foremost, we plead with you to take three or four deep breaths as soon as you feel anxious or overwhelmed. Deep breathing will immediately calm you. Your body will begin to relax. Take as many deep breaths as you need. Remember that God is part of your every breath. He creates the breath within you. Remember, we angels, too, are only a breath away. When you remember to breathe, you are more able to talk to God and us. Then you can begin to voice your fears and to ask for our help. Many times, part of your fear and anxiety is that you are trying to accomplish everything on your own. You were not created to be alone or to accomplish everything on your own. God and the angels are here for you and are waiting for you to call upon us for help. God has also provided people in your life to help you. Sharing your fears and anxious thoughts with others is not a sign of weakness. It is, in fact, a sign of strength. When you lay your worries on the table, it weakens the hold they have on your mind and your body. When you tell God and the angels what is troubling you, you begin to release the anxious feelings you are having. When you hold on tight to what makes you anxious, the stronger the feelings become. Soon you become overwhelmed and do not know where to turn.

God and your angels will always listen and answer your prayers. However, there are trained professionals who will also listen and help. There are agencies that strive to help and offer services to people in need. These trained volunteers and counselors act as earth angels sent by God to assist others. God wants you to be happy and peaceful. You deserve help from God and the angels. Call on us today. Your happiness and well-being are part of our mission.

Love and heavenly blessings,
The Angelic Kingdom

Author Note

I have had times in my life when I felt very anxious. Financial worries or struggles with relationships kept me up many nights. When I began to give God and the angels, my fears and anxieties, I noticed I felt lighter and more at peace. It was not an overnight cure, but I did begin to feel better. It took practice and patience with myself. Each time I started to feel anxious, I would take three or four deep breaths. Deep breaths immediately calmed me. It is amazing how I forgot to truly breathe each day. As I talked to God, I would picture angels taking away the fear and anxiety and giving it to God. I pictured the angels taking away the cause of my anxiety. I allowed myself to trust in God and to feel at peace. I asked the angels to help, and surround me every day. I asked for help in big and little matters. The amazing miracle was that it worked!

Now, I ask for help each day and it is supplied for me. If I start to feel nervous or anxious, I immediately stop myself. I take time to breathe and ask for help from God and the angels. I am honestly more peaceful and less stressed then I could ever have imagined.

Action Steps

When you begin to feel anxious or overwhelmed, stop what you are doing and breathe. It is essential to take at least three deep breaths, but you can take as many as needed. Feel your body naturally calm down. Begin to talk to God. Tell him what you are feeling. If you are able, tell him what is making you nervous or anxious. Now close your eyes and picture yourself, giving your fears to God or the angels. Visualize God or the angels, taking these fears to heaven. Allow yourself to feel lighter and more at peace. Practice this often until it becomes a habit. The peaceful feeling you receive is truly worth the practice.

Affirmation

I am surrounded by God and my angels. I am at peace.

Prayer

Dear God, I ask you to help remind me to breathe deeply and to feel your presence with each breath I take. Help me to trust you to take away my fears and insecurities. Help me to live in peace as you have intended me to be. Thank you for your help. Amen

Journal Reflection

1. Take three deep breaths right now. How does your body feel? How do you feel?

2. Think about any fears or anxiety you are experiencing right now. What is the cause of these fears? Journal now what you are feeling. If you are not sure, ask God and the angels to help you.

3. Close your eyes and picture two angels surrounding you. Picture yourself giving the angels these fears, people, or the situations that are causing fear and anxiety. Picture the angels taking these away for you and putting them at the feet of God. Don't hold onto them! Do this as many times as you feel necessary. Trust that the angels are doing this for you.

4. What did you see? How do you feel now? Remember, this exercise can be repeated any time you feel anxious or fearful.

Archangel Gabriel, Archangel Jophiel and Archangel Ariel

Dearest One,

We want to introduce you to three archangels who serve God, people, animals, and nature. You may call upon them for help at any time and will feel their heavenly arms surrounding you with love, peace, and guidance. As with all Archangels, they have no limit of time or space and can help many people at one time. These three Archangels are very nurturing and very gentle.

Archangel Gabriel

Archangel Gabriel is the messenger angel. Angel means messenger, and Gabriel is the supreme messenger angel of God. Archangel Gabriel can be called upon for help with any written, verbal, or non-verbal communication. When called upon, Archangel Gabriel will ensure that the communication is given and received in a loving, gentle, and respectful manner. Archangel Gabriel will guide all parties involved to understand the meaning and intention behind the communication and to help solve any conflicts that may arise due to miscommunication or misinterpretation. Archangel Gabriel guides teachers, students, and writers. Archangel Gabriel encourages journal writing for all humans to express their thoughts, receive ideas and inspirations, and to release past hurts and emotions. Archangel Gabriel is known for strength and leadership skills and will guide and enhance these qualities in anyone who calls upon this great angelic being.

Archangel Jophiel

Archangel Jophiel is known for being the angel of beauty. Archangel Jophiel helps humans to see the beauty in and around all life on earth. Archangel Jophiel encourages all humans to enjoy nature and to breathe in the fresh air to invigorate, rejuvenate, and inspire their daily lives. Archangel Jophiel asks you to stop and smell the roses and enjoy all the beauty in creation. This beautiful Archangel also wishes for you to see the beauty in yourself and others. Call on Archangel Jophiel for patience and endurance as you work with God and the angels in bringing your dreams to fruition. Archangel Jophiel wants you to enjoy the gifts found in the present moments. If you wish to declutter or to improve your home or workspace, she is the perfect angel to assist you. This angelic being will help you sort, remove, and lovingly detach from items that no longer serve you. Archangel Jophiel will lovingly clear out old energy and bring in new, fresh, creative energy to your work or home environment.

Archangel Ariel

Archangel Ariel is known as the lioness of God and is often seen with lions around her. She is the angel of courage, perseverance, and confidence. She will happily bestow these qualities on anyone who calls upon her. Archangel Ariel will stand by anyone who requests help in standing up for their beliefs and in speaking and living their truth. Archangel Ariel will encourage you to follow your heart and welcome in new opportunities that will guide you on your spiritual path. Archangel Ariel is known as the abundance angel and will lovingly provide all you will need to be prosperous on your life journey. She knows that you will also share the prosperity you receive with others.

Love and heavenly blessings,
The Angelic Kingdom

Author Note

I have called on these three Archangels many times. Archangel Ariel has been by my side my whole life and has given me the courage to make major life changes. Archangel Jophiel worked with me to declutter my mind, home, and life from anything that was blocking my energy or had kept me distracted from what I was meant to do. Archangel Gabriel and Archangel Michael were my co-authors of this angelic book. Archangel Gabriel also led me to a publisher and guided me to two friends who offered to edit the work for me. Archangel Gabriel was instrumental in guiding my work not only as an author but also as a teacher. I called upon her many times when I worked on report cards, sent emails, or held parent-teacher conferences. As a teacher, I had to communicate the positive and not so positive progress of students or report to parents about incidents that have happened at school. Time and time again, I would call on Archangel Gabriel for assistance in these conversations and I was always amazed at how smoothly the process went and how all parties involved were on the same page.

Action Steps

Call on Archangel Ariel to welcome new opportunities and abundance in your life. Ask her to give you the courage to make important life choices that will improve and enhance your life. Call on Archangel Jophiel to enjoy the beauty around you and to live in the present moment. Ask her to help you declutter your home to clean out old energy and to bring in the new. Call on Archangel Gabriel to help you communicate with the people in your life and to use your leadership skills to serve others.

Affirmation

I am surrounded by loving Archangels who lovingly support me on my life path.

Prayer

Dear God and Archangels, thank you for all the love, guidance, support, and courage you give me on my life journey. I know that you will provide for all my spiritual, physical, and financial needs. Amen

Journal Reflection

1. Call on one of these powerful and loving Archangels to help you with a problem, a project, or to improve your life. What areas of your life need assistance right now?

2. Return to this journal page after a few days and reflect on how the Archangel has helped you.

Archangel Michael

Dearest One,

This page is dedicated to Archangel Michael. He is known to be one of the seven Archangels that stands guard in God's heavenly kingdom. He is also known as St. Michael. His name means "he who is like God." Those who have seen him describe him as very tall with long blonde hair. He is gentle yet firm when needed. He speaks swiftly in a commanding, yet calm manner. He is often pictured with a great sword and a shield.

Archangel Michael is the angel of protection. He protects humans physically and spiritually. He is powerful, and his sword will break cords of negativity around humans and situations that need divine assistance. Archangel Michael is the defender against evil. Michael is brave, courageous, and will stand guard wherever he is needed. He is the light that dispels darkness. He is the patron saint of police officers.

Archangel Michael is also the angel who lovingly helps humans to follow their life path. He will bring you signs, people, resources, and information that you need to follow the path God has planned for you. If you are struggling with knowing what path you should be on, he will work with God to help you find your way.

Archangel Michael can assist humans who are struggling with technology issues. He can aid in computer malfunctions or internet disruptions. He is the heavenly technology support system.

Archangel Michael has no limits of time and space. He can be in many parts of the world at one time. You should not fear that calling on him will take him from someone else in need. He is capable of helping hundreds of people at one time. Archangel Michael and his band of angels are ready to serve whenever they are called. You will know he is near if you feel a sense of protection and peace come upon you.

Although Archangel Michael is known for his great power and strength, he also has a great sense of humor. He can help people look at situations in a new light using laughter and love to heal.

Love and heavenly blessings,
The Angelic Kingdom

Author Note

I have a strong and personal bond with Archangel Michael. He is near me quite often during angel readings with clients and when I feel a sense of danger or fear. I know that when I call upon him, he is near me instantly. I feel very safe and protected when Michael is around me. Michael has great wisdom and has taught me many ways to cut chords of negativity, protect my home, work, and family, and has helped me enhance my abilities to see, hear, and invoke angelic help. He is my go-to angel!

Archangel Michael taught me a method called Vacuuming. We all collect negativity from television, movies, news sources, and other people. It is essential to clear away this negativity and fill our bodies with pure angel light of love, protection, and healing. I use the vacuuming technique on myself and clients. It is very powerful, healing, and relaxing. You can use the vacuuming method as many times as you would like. You can ask Archangel Michael to vacuum your entire body and mind, your car, your home, and your workplace.

Action Steps

• Call on Archangel Michael when you feel danger or uneasiness around you.

- Call on Archangel Michael to surround you with a bubble of blue protective light for protection against negativity or danger. Ask for protective light daily.
- Ask Archangel Michael to cut cords that energetically tie you to people or situations that are draining your energy or are negatively affecting you, your home, or your workplace. You can also help by using your hand like a hatchet and cut the energy around your body. Washing your hands after you have encountered a negative thinking person or have been involved in a negative situation can also cut cords.
- If you feel you need help finding your life path or need guidance on what the next steps are for you, call on Archangel Michael for guidance. You will get ideas, signs, or suggestions through your intuition, through other people, or will get confirmation through some form of communication like TV, books, the radio, or mailings.
- Ask Archangel Michael to vacuum your home, car, workplace, or your body.

Body Vacuuming

1. Find a spot where you can sit quietly for at least 30 minutes.

2. Light a candle.

3. Breathe deeply several times.

4. Call on Archangel Michael to come to you. Ask for a Vacuuming.

5. Then close your eyes. Archangel Michael will use what looks like a vacuum. He will begin inside your body with your brain. He will circle around your brain, going through every crevice. He will vacuum out the negativity that looks like a blackish-gray material that has accumulated in areas of your body. He

will finish your brain and head and move to your parts of your face. He will go around and behind your eyes, your ears, mouth, nose, and cheeks.

6. He will vacuum down your throat and neck. He will vacuum around your shoulders. Then Archangel Michael will continue vacuuming down the front of your body. He will focus on every organ and in spots that seem to accumulate more debris like fingertips, knees, elbows, and toes.

7. Then he will vacuum down the back of your body. He will start at your brainstem and go through each and each vertebra of your back. He will continue down your body to the bottoms of your feet.

8. When the vacuuming is finished, he will switch off the vacuum and switch on a machine that will fill you up with angelic white light. It reminds me of white insulation foam. He will start in your brain and go down both sides of your body.

9. You will have a sense of knowing when it is complete. Sit quietly for a few more moments. Thank Archangel Michael for helping you. You may or may not see what is happening to you. It is perfect either way. You may also fall asleep while it is happening. That is perfect, as well.

You will feel relaxed and more at peace. After you have tried this technique several times, you can ask Archangel Michael to vacuum you as you sleep. Trust that it is done. You will sleep very well and very deeply.

Affirmation

I am safe, protected, and guided at all times.

Prayer

Dear God and Archangel Michael, thank you for lovingly protecting me and guiding me on my path of love and service. Amen

Journal Reflection

Set aside some quiet time for a vacuuming exercise with Archangel Michael. Spend time journaling your thoughts and feelings about the experience. How did it make you feel? Could you see anything as it happened? Did you hear or feel any messages for yourself?

Archangel Raphael

Dearest One,

This page is dedicated to Archangel Raphael. He is known to be one of the seven Archangels that stands guard in God's heavenly kingdom. He is also known as St. Raphael. His name means "God who heals." There are many stories and books describing miracles that have occurred with the intervention of Archangel Raphael. Archangel Raphael is surrounded by green light, which is a healing light. He is peaceful, gentle, and very compassionate. He is powerful, and his band of healing angels stand ready to serve whenever they are called. Archangel Raphael heals humans from physical, mental, and spiritual illnesses.

Archangel Raphael is the guardian of all who work in healing professions. He assists doctors, nurses, caretakers, and those who care for patients in a clinical setting. Archangel Raphael guides healers in the metaphysical fields. He works with Reiki and massage therapists, angel or psychic readers, and shamanic healers. Those who use crystals or oils for healing can count on him for choosing what is right for each client. Archangel Raphael inspires and guides scientists and researchers who are working on cures for human illnesses. He also works with anyone with addictions to help heal and end the addictions that plague their lives.

Archangel Raphael works with anyone who calls upon him. He has no limits of time and space. He can be in many parts of the world at one time. You should not fear that calling on him will take him from someone else in need. He is capable of helping hundreds of people at one time. Archangel Raphael works closely with Archangel Michael to bring healing, peace, and harmony to the world.

Archangel Raphael is known as the angel of travelers. Archangel Raphael guards and protects travelers and helps them reach their destination safely and provides for them along the way.

If you want to find a romantic partner, ask Archangel Raphael for help in this area. He is known for bringing partners together and removing any obstacles out of the way so they can begin their lives together.

Love and heavenly blessings,
The Angelic Kingdom

Author Note

I work very closely with Archangel Raphael when I am doing readings for clients or using Reiki to heal. He guides my hands as to where I should place them. He intuitively lets me know where a client needs more healing. He will provide messages for my clients on ways they can improve their health. I also call on Archangel Raphael to work with Archangel Michael when I use the Vacuuming technique for myself or clients. I describe the Vacuuming technique on the page dedicated to Archangel Michael. I often ask Archangel Raphael to send healing green light to flow through me from my head to my toes. I call upon him to send his green healing light to flow through or around my friends and family. I call upon him immediately if I hear of someone in an accident or the hospital. I know he will respond and surround those who are in need.

Archangel Raphael has asked me to picture green light around places that need healing. I have imagined healing green light stretching from the end of a country to another. Archangel Raphael told me that making this simple gesture is more powerful and healing than we can ever know. Visualizing green light can be used for a business, a school, a home, a city, or a country. Visualizing green light is one way we can all serve humankind with the help of the angels.

Archangel Raphael will help in little and big ways. One example happened once when I got a sliver in one of my fingers. I tried to get it out, and it went in deeper. I used tweezers and eventually gave up because I knew it would come to the surface in a day or two. After the third day of it still bugging me, it occurred to me that I hadn't asked for help from Archangel Raphael. So, I asked for help. In a matter of seconds, the sliver jumped from my finger and flew to my sink! It was amazing!

Action Steps

- Heal yourself by closing your eyes and ask Archangel Raphael to send green light through your entire body or concentrate on sending green light to an area of your body that needs more healing.
- Ask Archangel Raphael to send green light to friends or family that need healing. You can also picture green light surrounding your loved ones.
- Picture green healing light with Archangel Raphael's help to a place in the world that needs healing.
- Ask Archangel Raphael to help you with any addictions you may have.
- Ask Archangel Raphael to surround you with green light when you go on a trip.
- Ask Archangel Raphael to bring you a romantic partner that is blessed by heaven.

Affirmation

I am spiritually, emotionally, and physically healed.

Prayer

Dear God and Archangel Raphael, thank you for healing myself and those I love. Pour your loving, healing green light on our world. Please heal those who are suffering in mind and body. Thank you. Amen

Journal Reflection

Choose to experience one or more of the action steps. Reflect and journal on your experiences with Archangel Raphael.

Are Angels Real?

Dearest One,

We are more real than you can imagine. We are closer to you than you realize. Breathe. We are only a breath away. We are real and eager to help you know us, hear us, and call on us whenever you need assistance or guidance. There are hundreds of stories about us in books, blogs, movies, and the Internet. Stories of angels go back as far as the beginning of time, for God created us for the sole purpose of serving God and serving humankind. Your soul was created to experience love and life. We too, are created to help you learn, love, and experience all that your soul desires.

In the Angelic Kingdom, there are thousands of angels that serve many purposes. There are guardian angels, nature angels, water angels, and earth angels who have many different roles and purposes on earth. Angels are in every aspect of human, plant, and animal life. The angels follow God's commands and act as bridges between heaven and earth.

There is a special group of angels called the Archangels. Archangels are very wise, and their messages and counsel are valuable beyond measure. The Archangels have many angels in their charge. Archangels are not limited by time and space. Archangels can be with many people at the same time. They are powerful and carry out the mission of God in many ways. These angelic beings are mentioned in many religious texts, depicted in art forms, and found in many cultures around the world.

Guardian Angels are angels that are assigned to each human from the beginning of their time on earth to the end of their time on your beautiful planet. Their job is to guide you and assist you on your earthly journey. They are always by your side and wait for your invitation. All angels respect your free will and will not interfere unless you ask for their help.

Archangels and angels are loving beings who wish to help all humans to live in peace, harmony, and to fulfill their purpose on the earthly plane.

Love and heavenly blessings,
The Angelic Kingdom

Author Note

I call on the archangels and angels every day! Some archangels serve as guardians of protection, abundance, romance, travel, and even transition from this life to the next. I encourage you to call on your guardian angels daily for help and guidance. I also encourage you to call on the archangels for their help. They are powerful and can and will bring God's miracles into your life. It does not matter how you call on them. It matters that you do call on them. You can speak directly to a guardian angel or directly to a particular archangel. You can simply say, "Angels," and they are ready and willing to hear your requests and take your prayers to God.

You can also mention your guardian angels by name. You can simply ask what their name is, and they will reveal it to you. I learned who my guardian angels were over fifteen years ago. I was attending a workshop on angels. I wanted to learn all I could and was fascinated by all the information presented to me. The speaker was an international expert on angels, and the presentation was informative and life-changing. The speaker asked us to practice the information we were learning by completing several activities during the workshop. One of the activities was to ask our guardian angels to tell us their names. There were over hundred people at this conference asking their angels for their names and for signs that they heard correctly. I quietly asked my angels to tell me their names. The first name I heard was "Bob." I didn't think I had heard correctly. I have a brother named Bob. Perhaps, I was thinking of him. I asked again. The name "Bob" came to my mind again. The speaker told us not to put much thought into what we were hearing. Just to hear and trust. I asked for the third time. I heard "Bob" very loudly!

The next angel name that came to me was Archangel Ariel. I couldn't believe that an archangel would be my guardian angel. Archangels are high-level beings! However, that was the name I heard. I asked for some signs to show me that I was hearing her correctly. I did not hear anything at first. I learned that Archangel Ariel was the angel of abundance and the angel of courage. She is often pictured with lions around her. After the workshop ended several hours later, I traveled home. I did not reach my home until after midnight. I was very tired and just wanted to crawl into bed. However, I had this feeling that I was supposed to look at this stuffed animal I had in the corner of my room. The animal is Leo the Lion. I am a Leo, and the lion was a cute gift to remind me of my astrological sign. I picked up the lion and smiled. Then I went to bed. The next day, I went to my parent's home. My mom asked me to get an antique lion made of iron down from a shelf. She said she wanted to give it to my nephew for Christmas. Later that day, I was watching a TV show, and there was a commercial with a lion on it. Suddenly, the light bulb above my head went off! Archangel Ariel is surrounded by lions! She had sent me three signs!

I learned a lot of lessons from that workshop. First, I learned that archangels can be guardian angels and will send you signs if you ask. The second lesson I learned was that angels have heavenly, as well as earthly names, like the name Bob. The third lesson I learned was the most important one of all, to trust what I hear. Trust and believe!

Action Steps

Spend some time sitting quietly in a place where you will not be disturbed for at least fifteen minutes. Ask your guardian angels what their names are. If you wish, ask them to show you a sign that you heard correctly. Write down the two names that you hear. Is there a name that makes your heart jump? Is there a name that sounds so familiar to you, or is it a favorite name of yours? Often, clients will tell me that they remember calling a stuffed animal or an imaginary playmate by the same name they heard for their guardian angel. That is because their imaginary playmate and their guardian angel may be one and the same!

Affirmation

I am open and receptive to the messages from God and my angels.

Prayer

Dear God, I thank you for creating angels to watch over us and to guide us. Help me to listen and follow your messages of love and guidance. Amen

Journal Reflection

Call on your guardian angels for an issue you are facing right now. Journal what that issue is. Sit quietly for a few minutes and open your heart to hear the messages your angels are sending you. Watch and listen for more signs and messages in the days to come. Journal what you feel, see, hear, and experience.

Balance In Your Life

Dearest One,

When you are feeling distracted, forgetful, or worried, it is most likely because you are not in balance. We angels know the benefits of staying in balance. Think of a scale where the balance point is in the middle. Think of one side as your career, job, tasks at home, yard work, or schoolwork. Think of the other side as fun, time for yourself, time with family, relaxation, or quiet time. Which way does your balance lean? In more cases than not, the side for fun is much lighter. When you are in balance with yourself and your world, your body, emotions, mind, and health become balanced as well. Oh, we hear you already saying, but I have this to do and that to do. Yes, we know you have many responsibilities, and we honor that. However, we also know that we can lighten your responsibilities if you call upon us. We also know that all work and no play is not healthy. We encourage you to take time throughout the day and week for balance. Even a small amount can have a significant impact on your health and mood. Exercise is an excellent way to get in shape and balance. Meditation helps balance your mind, body, and spirit. Spending time with loved ones and friends will also bring your life fun, fulfillment, and balance.

Take some time today to reflect on which way your balance tilts. Ask the angels to assist you in balancing your life. The benefits of living a balanced life will promote a happy and healthy lifestyle for years to come.

Love and heavenly blessings,
The Angelic Kingdom

Author Note

I think I learned what it means to be in balance, best from my parents. My dad was a labor worker and accountant. He was a husband and father to eight children. He worked hard each day at a factory, came home and did chores inside and outside of the home, and always had time for play. My mom was a housewife, as well as a working mom for many years. She volunteered at church and our school. She spent her days taking care of us, sewing, cooking, baking, and helping us with homework. We would play baseball as a family, play frisbee, play croquet, or other yard games. We would play cards or other board games at night and especially on Sundays. My parents knew the value of family time and fun. They believed it was important to take family vacations to see the great country we live in or to see local interests not far from our home. My mom and dad would also take vacations as a couple. They knew they needed time together to keep their relationship strong and happy.

My brothers and sisters keep these traditions alive by going on vacations, enjoying amusement parks, playing indoor and outdoor games, and enjoying sporting events. We like to hike and spend time in local, state, and national parks. We are instilling these values in our nieces and nephews.

Balance can be as simple as reading a book, talking with a friend on the phone, watching a show that makes you laugh, or sitting outside and relaxing. Balance doesn't have to cost a lot of money, but the benefits are priceless!

Action Steps

- Spend some time in prayer.
- Meditate.
- Talk to the angels.
- Read a book or a magazine.
- Join a yoga class.

- Walk daily.
- Read something inspirational each day.
- Take deep breaths throughout the day to fill your body with much-needed oxygen and relaxation.
- Call a friend or meet for dinner.
- Write in a journal.
- Work in a garden.
- Sit in the sun and enjoy the warmth.
- Go fishing.
- Go hiking in a forest. Notice the many kinds of green plants and trees you encounter.
- Play cards with friends or family members.
- Play a board game.
- Sit and listen to some music.
- Go to a movie or watch one on TV.
- Go on a picnic.
- Sit by a lake.

Affirmation

I am balanced and aligned with God's plan for me.

Prayer

Dear God, help me to instill balance in my life. When I am in balance, I am more able to align with my true purpose. With your help, I can align my spirit, mind, and body. Amen

Journal Reflection

1. Spend a few minutes, reflecting on what a typical day or week looks like for you.

2. We encourage you to create a list titled "Work" and another list titled "Play." Write down as many items as you can think of that you have experienced in a day or a week.

3. Look at your list. What does it show you? Remember, there is no judgment. What can you do to make your list and your life more balanced? Which items on your list bring you joy? Which items on your list could you ask for the angel's help?

4. Journal how you will add more balance to your life.

Call On Us

Dearest One,

Many humans are afraid to call on angels for help. Many people are worried that they are not asking for God's help if they call upon us. Yet, we are created by God and, in turn, are one with God. God is in us as he is in each of you. God has empowered us to help you with your human and spiritual journeys. That is why you have guardian angels surrounding you, guiding you, and protecting you. We are beings of light and love. Our messages are also filled with light and love. We ask you not to pray to us. God is the heavenly father to turn to in prayer

We ask that you do not let fear keep you from our love and our loving messages for you. Some people are afraid that we will only give them messages of doom and gloom. They are afraid that we will tell them something bad is going to happen to them or their loved ones. Nothing could be further from the truth! Our guidance and wisdom will encourage you to make healthy choices or to make life changes that will help you on your life journey and to increase your joy and happiness. Others feel they do not deserve our help or love. Some of you feel that you have made too many mistakes, or your past decisions should keep us from you. If you could see yourself as we do, you would know that we understand your mistakes as learning opportunities. There is no judgment. We are here for all people, no matter where you are on your journey. It does not matter if you are religious or not. All people deserve our love and light. God has given us this mission, and we lovingly carry out our duties daily.

There are angels assigned to everyone and every human vocation and job. Angelic beings take care of the oceans and rivers, flowers, and trees. The animal kingdom is surrounded by special angels who watch over them and protect them. Some angels are assigned to watch over your homes and cars. Angelic support surrounds you when you are grieving for a loved one. There are even angels that help you to learn and to understand new concepts and skills.

When you call on us, you are invoking divine help and assistance. You are asking God and the angels to help you and to provide people, materials, or ideas to help you in any circumstance. Call on us and know that we are only a breath away. Our mission is to help you live out your mission. Call on us daily and notice the miracles that happen in your life.

Love and heavenly blessings,
The Angelic Kingdom

Author Note

I cannot even begin to explain what a difference, angels have made in my life. I am becoming a much more patient and peaceful person. My faith in God and my awareness of the gifts God brings has increased tenfold. I notice miracles happening all the time. The angels have opened my eyes to all the wonders and beauty that God has and is creating. The angelic kingdom has made me more aware of what I can and will accomplish with them by my side. It has allowed me to open my gifts and to share them with others. I know my mission is to hear angelic messages and to deliver the messages to other people. It is an honor to do so.

When I first began to see and listen to angels, I was honored yet also humbled. I questioned why they chose me? What made me special? What is my mission? Does God want me to do this? What if I am not hearing them correctly? Will others believe me? I now know that was my fear and my ego talking to me. I also know that I do have a wonderful gift, and it is my mission to share it with others. I also know that angels talk to everyone if we choose to listen.

One day I asked the angels why I was chosen for this divine mission. The message I received stated that I am part of a circle that includes them. I help bring their messages to others. If I did not fulfill my role, the ring is broken. They have their missions and jobs to do as well. They need me and others like me to help carry out God's will and plans for the world. They are indeed God's messengers, and they joyously and lovingly help people, animals, and all of God's creation to live and love harmoniously in our world.

Action Steps

The next time you are faced with a problem or a situation, call on the angels to help you with it. No problem or situation is too big or too small for the angels to help. You simply call out to them in your mind or out loud and then trust that it is heard. Then watch and see what happens. I encourage you to make this a daily habit. Thank God and the angels for their help. You will notice better days and things falling into place for you. Your job is to ask.

Affirmation

I am in constant communication with God and my Angels. I am grateful for their messages.

Prayer

Dear God, help me ask for and receive your help in all areas of my life. Help me to allow your divine mission to work through me to help others and myself to learn, live, and love. Amen

Journal Reflection

Reflect and journal on the following questions. How do I feel about angels? How do I feel about receiving help from God and the angels? Do I have any fears about receiving their support? Do I believe I deserve their help?

Clutter Free Homes and Workspaces

Dearest One,

Clutter can impact your energy and stress levels. When you declutter your home and workspace, you will see your energy levels rise, you will think clearly, and you will feel happier and more at peace. It is a world that sends a message of more, but your mind and body crave less and less. It is fine to buy new things, but we suggest then that you give away some old items. There are some suggestions we offer to help you feel happier and more at peace.

- When you buy a new item of clothing, donate three other items from your closet.
- When you decide to declutter your house, we suggest that you think little before big. If you look at a whole room or an entire closet to clean, it can overwhelm you, and you may not even start. Instead, focus on one corner of a room or one shelf of a closet. One corner or one shelf is doable and you will feel a sense of accomplishment after it is complete.
- Call on the angels to help you detach from items you do not use or need.
- If you have not worn an item for several years, it is time to let it go.
- Take your items to a homeless shelter or charity to donate.
- Take your items to a consignment shop to resell.
- Play some uplifting music as you declutter. Music helps you move and think faster. It lifts your mood and your productivity.
- In your workspace, take notice of boxes that can be moved or gone through that are not needed anymore. Free up the space around your desk or work area.
- If you have a desk or cubicle, make it a daily habit to file or shred any papers you do not need.

- Go through your emails. Trash any emails that you do not need.
- Make use of file drawers or file bins that help you stay organized and neat and tidy.

We guarantee that you will feel and think better when you begin to declutter. You will feel your stress levels decrease, and your energy levels increase. Isn't that worth a few hours of your time each week?

Love and heavenly blessings,
The Angelic Kingdom

Author Note

I would like to share some experiences I have had with decluttering. During one of my angel readings with a client, I suggested that she call on Archangel Jophiel to declutter. Archangel Jophiel is the angel of beauty. She will help you to see the beauty in yourself and your surroundings. She is joyful and purposeful.

One day, I was giving an angel card reading for a client. I drew Archangel Jophiel's card from an angel card deck. I showed the card to the client and then replaced it in the card deck. The next day I woke up and felt the urge to clean out a closet. I had not planned on cleaning a closet that day and was not in a mood to do that. However, the urge was quite strong. I got dressed and went out to the dining room. There on the table was Archangel Jophiel's card! I know I put it away the night before. I was asked to get out three bags. One for donation, one for garbage, and one for items to give to friends or family members. I began to clean like crazy. I could feel Archangel Jophiel helping me to decide what to keep and what to give away. In less than two hours, the closet was cleaned, and I had three bags to take to a charity.

Action Steps

Here are some other suggestions I have found helpful in decluttering. I have used them all and have encouraged others to use them as well.

- Call on Archangel Jophiel to help you beautify your home and to help you declutter and clean.
- Make a game out of decluttering. Set a timer for fifteen minutes. Tell yourself that you are going to put twenty things away in that time. It is incredible how much you can do, and you will already see a cleaner room. Using this technique often energizes me, and I set the timer again and put twenty more things away.
- Don't declutter alone! If you live alone, ask some friends to come over and help you. You can talk with your friends and get a lot done at the same time. You can repay them with supper or help them declutter one afternoon. If you have a family, they should help! Kids love to help and clean up when we make it a game. Often, children love to clean but are usually not given a chance, or the adults want to do it just to get it done. At times, adults need to loosen the reins and let the children help. It may not always be perfect or just the way we want it to be, but it will help lessen the load and instill a good work ethic and good character traits. Have each family member put away twenty items in the correct space. Think about how much can be accomplished in a short amount of time.
- As you are watching TV, put away as many items as you can during the commercials.
- Clean out one drawer or shelf as you play music or watch TV. During a commercial, grab another drawer to declutter.
- When you have bags or items to take to a consignment shop, put them in your car right away. If possible, take them to

the donation place that same day. The energy will begin to shift in your home and car.

- A good rule of thumb is if you didn't know the item was in the dresser or closet, you probably don't need it. You haven't used it, so why keep it?
- I used to keep clothes for when I could fit in them again. I have decided not to do that anymore for several reasons. I may or may not lose weight right away, and when I do lose it, I will want new clothes for the new body I created. So, why keep the old clothes when others can use them?
- I heard a statement years ago that always stays in my mind when I need to declutter a room or my home. The statement asked the reader to reflect on the following scenario. Imagine that if you were to lose all your possessions in a fire or a tornado, which items would you not miss or replace? Those items are the first items that can be donated. It also helps you to detach from any emotions you have for those items.

Affirmation

I am living and working in a peaceful, energetic, and stress -free environment.

Prayer

Dear God and Archangel Jophiel, help me to declutter my home and workspace so that I can hear your guidance and to work more productively. Help me to declutter so that I can live a more peaceful, energetic, and stress-free life. Thank you for your love, guidance, and assistance. Amen

Journal Reflection

Spend some time thinking about the clutter in your home or office. Spend some time journaling on the following questions. What needs to declutter first? What is stopping you from decluttering? Is there anyone you can call on to help? How can you break down the decluttering to more manageable steps?

Count Your Blessings

Dearest One,

There are so many reasons to be thankful. God has blessed you with many gifts. One of the greatest gifts he has given you is the gift of angels. Each of you has two guardian angels with you at all times. These special angels guide you and protect you every single day. You can ask God for more angels to surround you any time you wish.

Look around you right now. What are you thankful for in this moment? God and the angels ask you to notice these blessings and to be grateful for them. It is not that God and the angels need to be thanked or recognized for their gifts. It is because when you recognize the blessings you receive and are grateful for them, you become more open and receptive to new blessings and gifts.

When you are amid sadness, illness, or having a rough day, counting your blessings can immediately change your vibration to a happier, more positive one. Counting your blessings can create a happier environment for you as well as the people who surround you.

We encourage you to notice your blessings throughout the day and to think of them before you sleep. We guarantee you will sleep better and wake up refreshed.

Love and heavenly blessings,
The Angelic Kingdom

Author Note

We have all heard the phrase "an attitude of gratitude" is the way we should live our lives. It is very true and emphasized by the angels. It is a habit that should be practiced often. I always thank God for the many blessings in my life before I go to bed each night. However, I have also begun the practice of thanking God several times a day. This practice has made me feel happier and more at peace in so many ways. It may be something small like hearing a baby giggle, and immediately it makes me smile. I may see a rainbow and thank God for the blessings of promises filled and the joy and beauty a rainbow brings to the world. Recognizing my blessings has opened new doors for me and allowed me to invite in more blessings and miracles. Thanking God at the moment, and recognizing the blessings at that moment, helps me to live in the present. It reminds me that God is with me all through my day and night. I am never alone.

Action Steps

Thank God each day for five blessings in your life. The next day add three more blessings to your grateful list. Notice how your body and mind react to your recognition of your many blessings and gifts. Keeping a gratitude journal is a beautiful way to recognize blessings and to add new ones that God brings into your life.

Affirmation

I am truly blessed in all ways.

Prayer

Dear God, thank you for the many blessings and gifts you have bestowed on me and my loved ones. I am truly grateful, and I share my gifts with others knowing there is abundance for all. Amen

Journal Reflection

Reflect on five blessings you have in your life. Thank God for those blessings. Journal why you are grateful for the blessings God has given you. Each day, take some time to reflect and journal on three more blessings you recognize God has given you.

Create Your Own Story

Dearest One,

Often, we hear humans wonder why their lives are moving along in a way that is not what they wanted or expected. "Why is this happening to me?" "Why do some people find love, and I don't?" "Will I be stuck in this dead-end job forever?" "How do I change my life and the direction it is going?"

Have you ever thought that maybe it is time to rewrite or create a new story for yourself? Yes, you have the power to do so. You are faced with many choices during your life time. Often it may seem as if choices are made for you; however, you can and do make many choices that determine your life every day. You are a creator, along with God. When you take action steps, the universe offers in kind. When you decide what it is you truly desire, ask for it, and take action steps towards it, you will create and live the story you are dreaming about. We encourage you to take some quiet time to rewrite your story. This exercise will create great benefits for you and bring you the life you desire and deserve.

- Sit quietly. Grab some paper and a pen. Begin to answer the following questions to help you rewrite or create your story. You can write or draw your answers.
- What would make you happy and fulfilled?
- What is your profession in your new story? What is your salary?
- What would you like your work situation to be?
- How are your finances and money situation?
- Where are you living?
- Who are the people in your life? Who do you want to bring into your life?

- How do you feel? How is your health?
- What do you like to do for fun? What are your hobbies?

Review your story often and revise it if necessary. See it in your mind. Feel it! Tell others that you trust and who will encourage you and cheer on your new story. Avoid people who do not believe in your new story or want to keep you in your own story to benefit their reasons and agendas. Believe in miracles and the power you have to create and manifest. Step out of your old story and into the new!

Love and heavenly blessings,
The Angelic Kingdom

Author Note

I have received guidance from the angels on many occasions to rewrite my story. I refined my story often and added new elements when needed. My story changed, and I began to change, as well. These changes helped me realize that some people wanted to keep me in my old story. The old story would benefit them, but it did not benefit me. As I changed the energy around me, I noticed that the people around me also began to change. I began to speak of my new life even if it wasn't entirely true yet. I politely corrected others who still wanted to see me in the old story. I kindly told them that my life was changing, and I was heading in a new direction. As I changed, so did their perceptions of me. The incredible miracle is that when you change for the better, so do the people around you. We are all one. When we do something good for ourselves and our lives, we also help others to change and better their lives as well.

I was single for over thirty years. As a teacher, people were used to calling me Miss and thought that was my story. It was not the story I wanted. I wanted to marry and share my life with a wonderful spouse. I took action steps to create the story I wanted to live. I began to visualize the kind of man I wanted to meet and what qualities he possessed. I pictured myself dating, getting engaged, and getting married. I created the story I wanted to live.

Action Steps

When I encourage people to rewrite their personal stories, they like the idea but find starting overwhelming. Your new story may be written in the form of a list or a paragraph. There is no wrong or right way to rewrite your story. Give yourself some quiet time when you know you will not be disturbed. Then begin to type or write down ideas on what you want to change in your life. Remember to think about big changes and possibilities. Do not limit yourself. Remember, God and the universe are unlimited, and so are the gifts God can bring into your life. Take time each day to read and pray over your new story. Rewrite or add changes to your story. There is no limit on how long or short your unique story is. There is no limit to how many changes or possibilities you include in your story. If you feel stuck, ask the angels to help guide your ideas and writing. They will be happy to do so.

The key is to get started and put energy towards it. Then the angels will begin to work on your behalf. You may need to take additional action steps to not only create your new story but to bring it into reality. Action steps may be updating a resume, starting a workout routine, joining a new class, or whatever you feel guided to do. Trust your intuition and feelings and act on them. Think of all that you can and will gain by spending some quality time with yourself. You are the star of your story!

Affirmation

I am changing my life for the better.

Prayer

Dear God, I know it is time to make changes in my life. I know I deserve a truly loving and fulfilling life. Help me create a new story for myself. Help me to take the action steps necessary to bring my new story into existence. I know that all things are possible. Amen

Journal Reflection

1. Take some quiet time to think about what you want your story to be.

2. Write down some words, phrases, or sentences that describe your new story.

3. Then ask God to bring in your new story.

Dance and Sing!

Dearest One,

Dancing and singing are two beautiful ways to connect with your body and your soul. Music lifts your soul and your body to higher levels and realms. Music is powerful and a true gift from God.

Listening to music enables you to feel every emotion and experience life in many different ways. A song can bring back memories or start new ones. We encourage you to sing a song. Let the words and music fill you up. When you sing, you feel good. When you sing, your soul has a voice!

When you dance, your true self emerges. You feel free, and your body naturally flows with the music. Put on your favorite music and let your body dance and sway to the rhythm. Don't worry about how you look or what the proper steps are. Just enjoy the music and the movement. Feel and experience your body and soul come alive.

Music and dancing are happening in nature all around you. Listen to the beautiful songs the birds are singing. The wind sings a song as it blows through the trees. The rain makes a song with a pitter patter. Butterflies dance from flower to flower. Bees communicate with dance. Dancing and singing are everywhere. Join in the beautiful rhythm of life!

Love and heavenly blessings,
The Angelic Kingdom

Author Note

Dancing and singing are truly natural ways for our bodies to move and to express ourselves. It is also a great way to exercise and have fun! At times, it is good to get out of our comfort zones and try something new. I took a belly dancing class and loved it! It was a great way to exercise and to feel very feminine. I enjoyed it so much; I took the class three years in a row! A few years later, I was asked to join a singing group. I had not sung with a choir since high school and was feeling apprehensive about my skill level. I received a message from the angels that joining this group would be a wonderful thing for me to do. I did join, and I really enjoyed singing and learning new music. Often, I like to put on some of my favorite music and just dance. It is a good workout and I just feel happier.

I would like you to think about children in terms of dancing and singing. They naturally love to sing and dance. They love to be sung too. We immediately smile when a baby begins to dance. Many toys and games have music built in for children to enjoy. I taught first graders for over thirty years. They loved to sing and dance! What they loved, even more, was for their teacher to dance and sing with them. We used music in the classroom to practice math facts or to remember new concepts. We would get up and dance for a brain break after a morning of learning. I had as much fun as they did!

Action Steps

I encourage you to listen to your favorite music. Move your body to the music. Do not worry if you are a good or a bad dancer. Just move! Feel how the music moves your body. Dancing is great to do when you need an energy boost, or you are feeling sad or down. It can be as simple as dancing to the music during a commercial break. Many commercials play upbeat songs or music that encourages us to get up and move.

If you are trying to learn new material, repeat the material to yourself or orally as you move. The movement will help you incorporate the new content into your brain.

If you are feeling stuck or want to shift your energy or your way of thinking, use movement to do this. You will feel an energy shift and feel lighter in just a few minutes.

Dancing and singing are truly natural ways for our bodies to move and to express ourselves. It is also a great way to exercise and have fun!

Affirmation

I am happy and healthy. I dance with the rhythm of life.

Prayer

Dear God, help me to move my body. Help me to feel the joy that music brings. Help me to remember and use the healing benefits of music in all aspects of my life. Thank you for your help. Amen

Journal Reflection

Think about the last time you danced or sang with the radio. How did you feel? Do you sing at church or to your children? Do you go to concerts or hear a band at a club? What songs make you happy? What songs make you dance or sway to the music?

Take some time to journal your thoughts about music, singing, and dancing.

Death

Dearest One,

Death is not an ending. It is a transition, and it heralds new beginnings. Death, as you see it in your human world, is all around you. It is happening all the time in many different ways. There is no need to fear it. There are many examples of death or, as we prefer to call it, transitions in your world. Leaves fall off trees and plants wither and die. People change jobs or move to new places. Students finish one grade and move to the next grade level. A child grows up and becomes an adult. People retire and begin a new phase of their lives. A couple ends their relationship. There are growth, change, and blessings in each of these examples.

We are not trying to diminish your pain or hurt when a loved one transitions or dies. You will and should grieve. It is part of your human experience. We wish you to think of this as not an ending of a relationship with your loved one. It is a transition for them and you. Love can never die. The bonds of love bind you in this world and the next. When a loved one transitions, it is because they have completed and accomplished all that they were to do in this lifetime. They have learned and taught lessons to those they met along their journey of life. Yes, it is even so, for when a little one passes. All transitions bring new beginnings and new blessings. When you think of death as a transition, as a time to learn, as a time for blessings, and as a time of teaching others, you will begin to feel more peace and acceptance in your life. Your loved ones are not leaving you. They are transitioning to a place of great love. They are very close and are supporting you as you continue your journey of love and learning in this world and the next.

Love and heavenly blessings,
The Angelic Kingdom

Author Note

Many clients come to me, hoping to communicate with loved ones who have passed on. They are longing for that connection again. We long to hear the voices of our passed loved ones, hold them again, and say all the things we wish we would have said. The truth is we haven't lost that connection. They are still with us. They are closer to us than we can imagine. The great news is that we can talk to them anytime or anywhere! We don't need to visit their gravesite or wait for a special holiday or anniversary. They love us, and they are with us in all aspects of our lives.

Several years ago, I had an angel reading done by a good friend of mine. She said that my grandmother was coming through to say hello. My grandmother had passed when I was only four. I have very few memories of her. My friend said that my grandmother had been with me while I had been teaching that day. My grandmother told my friend in detail the things she had seen and heard me say in my classroom that afternoon. It was amazing! It was then that I realized how close deceased loved ones are to us.

Often, clients will state that they believe a deceased loved one had come to them in a dream or that they saw them at the end of their bed. Clients are afraid that this may only be their imagination. It is not your imagination. Deceased loved ones do come to us in dreams, visions, or visitations. It is quite common.

A few nights before my dad transitioned or passed away, he appeared with an angel above my bed. The experience was quite clear and very real. I reached out to him and called out his name. I knew I was not dreaming. A few days later, he left this world. That visitation told me that his transition would be soon and that he would be okay. It also confirmed to me that I would be okay as well. It was very comforting.

Clients will often report seeing cardinals or butterflies around when they are thinking of a deceased loved one. Cardinals and butterflies are signs from loved ones that have passed. My family and

I have had several messages from the bird kingdom. We truly believe they are messages from my dad. My dad passed away several years ago. My mom loves to see cardinals in the yard. There are times that a cardinal will peck at our dining room window several times. The window is right where my dad's chair used to be. Hummingbirds can also be signs given to us by loved ones who have crossed over. One day, I went to see my brother and his family. They were trying to get a trapped hummingbird out of their house. The bird flew all around the living room and dining room. I noticed that there was a puzzle set up on a table. My dad loved puzzles! I told my brother that I had a feeling that the hummingbird was a sign from Dad. Suddenly, the hummingbird landed on the puzzle. It stayed on the puzzle for several seconds then flew out the door. We knew Dad had visited us!

Action Steps

Make a list of the transitions you have experienced in the last few months or years. Recall what feelings you had at the time of each transition. How have your feelings changed? How have you changed? What lessons or blessings have you experienced? Can you see how God has been with you through all these transitions? Write down what you can remember. Add more to the list as feelings or memories come back to you. Make this a practice for you. You will begin to feel more peaceful and less anxious when new transitions occur in your lifetime.

Affirmation

I am surrounded by God and the angels as I experience endings or deaths in my life. Deceased loved ones are still with me and are loving me as I continue my journey.

Prayer

Dear God, help me to see your work and love in every transition I face. Help me to see the blessings in each situation. When I am faced with the loss of a loved one, please help me to lean on you for love and support. Please help me to realize that my loved ones are still near me. Help me to remember that I can feel them and talk to them at all times. I am grateful for your help and guidance. Amen

Journal Reflection

1. Reflect on the transitions you have experienced in your lifetime. How did you get through each transition?

2. Are you going through any transitions now? A new job? A divorce? Ask the angels for help as you make these transitions.

3. Have you had any loved ones cross over? Spend some time talking to them. Trust that they hear you. You can speak to them anytime and anywhere. Take time to journal your feelings after your experiences.

4. Trees become dormant during the winter months. Has the death of a loved one caused you to remain dormant as well? Is it time for you to live and explore life again?

Faith

Dearest One,

You have heard it said that faith can move mountains. We tell you faith can and does move mountains. You may have also heard it said, without faith, you have nothing. Faith is the driving force to keep you on your journey. Today, we would like to push your current understanding of faith farther.

Faith in God is all you need. Yet, how many times do you as humans choose not to believe or let your faith be shaken by news broadcasts or other's opinions? God makes the world spin every day. He makes the sun come up in the morning for you to see. He makes the seasons change. Do you not think he can help you with all your worries and struggles? Do you not believe he can help make all your dreams come true? Trust in God and in the angels to help you with all things big or small.

Have faith that your prayers have been heard and answered. The angels will take your prayers and lay them before God. Yes, God knows what you want before you ask, but it is still important to ask. Asking is the first step. Then let heaven take care of the rest.

Your job is to ask and have faith that everything will be okay. Let go and let God! Often, humans stand in their own ways of having their prayers answered. Let God answer your prayers. He will answer your prayers in ways you are not able to imagine. Have faith and know that God has only the best planned for his dear children. Your faith can and does move mountains. Remember, with God and the angels on your team, you are unstoppable!

Love and heavenly blessings,
The Angelic Kingdom

Author Note

Since I began talking and listening to angels, I have noticed that my faith and trust in God has increased. I worry less, and I let God be the one in control. Calling on angels has brought me much peace and joy in my life. Giving up control is not always easy to do. There are times, I am very disappointed if things don't go my way or the way I thought they should. These are the times I know I need to step back and reflect on who really is in charge. Doesn't God know more than I? God does not have limits. Are my thoughts limiting how my dreams can come true? When I truly surrender and give my cares and problems to God, the problems are taken care of, and I am at peace. Surrendering takes practice, but the benefits are so worth it! When I ask, I often say with my prayer, "this or something better." God knows the best way to answer my prayers.

Action Steps

Visualize an angel standing before you ready to take your cares, problems, worries, and prayers to God. Then visualize the angel taking these to heaven and placing them before God. Leave them there! Do not take them back or hold onto them. When you hold onto them, they cannot be answered in the way that is best. As humans, we tend to be limited in our thinking. Yet, God has no limits. There is nothing he can and can't do. So lay your prayers before God and have faith that they will be answered. Watch the mountains move and know that God was behind it all.

Affirmation

I am able to give God all my cares. I believe and have faith that God will provide in ways greater than I can imagine.

Prayer

Dear God, I give you my cares and worries to take to heaven. I give you my prayers to be answered. I know that you will answer them. I have faith that you will dispel my worries and bring me peace. Help me to let go and let you lead my life. Thank you for your help and guidance. Amen

Journal Reflection

Reflect on your cares and worries you are facing right now. Spend time journaling or time writing a letter to God and the angels asking them to take your cares and worries to heaven. Then visualize the angels taking your concerns to heaven. Journal how you feel when you let go and let God take care of your needs.

Fear

Dearest One,

All humans have fear. How do you handle your fears? Do you hold onto them? Do you release them? If you hold on to them, they have the power. If you recognize the fear and then let it go, it has no power over you. Fears stem from past experiences, conversations with others, the unknown, and the "what if this happens" questions that go through your minds.

Fear is a natural emotion for humans to feel. Some fear is needed to warn you of danger or to promote safety for yourself or others. However, it can stop many of you from moving forward or from trying something new. Remember that God is love, and he will never let you fall. He is always there. He is a loving parent guiding you in all ways. He knows that fears are lower based energies and that fears are not real. Only love is real. Breathe in and out slowly. Let white light fill your body from head to toe. Breathe out the fear. Let the angels take your fear and transmute the energy for you. Let go of the fear and trust that God will always be with you, keeping you safe and secure in his love.

Love and heavenly blessings,
The Angelic Kingdom

Author Note

Since I began talking and listening to my angels, I have been able to let go of some fears that kept me from doing some things I wanted to do or discouraged by others to do. I now trust that my angels are surrounding me, and I do not have to live in fear. I call on the angels to help and surround me every day. They are happy to do so. I ask that they take away my fears, and help me face new fears that may develop. The angels are happy to help with those requests. It is an exchange that is so worthwhile. I give them my fears and they fill me with peace. I also try to avoid negative people, news items, or shows that create fear. These types of TV shows or people create fear to entertain, promote their own agendas, or to create more drama. This drama can create a fear-based community. Of course, not all news items or shows create fear or negativity. However, it is best to limit how much fear or negativity is surrounding you. Living a fearful or negative thinking existence can begin to create "dis-ease" in your mind and body. Know and believe that you are protected and surrounded by heavenly light, and watch your fears disappear. Fear and negative thinking cannot survive in the light of God.

Action Steps

Take time to reflect on what fears you possess. List them if you like. Which ones are stronger than others? Are your fears due to something that has happened to you in the past? Are the fears concerning what the future holds? Have your fears been brought on by others? Choose one of the fears. Take a few moments to ask the angels to help you release the fear. Close your eyes and picture an angel taking your fear and laying it at the feet of God. Truly let God take it from you. God is happy to take these burdens from us. We just need to ask. Often, we have had the fear for a long time, and it has become part of us. You may need to practice this exercise several times until you truly feel you have let it go. This is a very powerful exercise, and it has helped many people, including myself. You can do this exercise as often as you wish with as many fears as you wish. You can also ask Archangel Michael to cut away the chords of fear and negativity. Notice how you begin to feel happier, lighter, and more at peace.

Affirmation

I am at peace, for God is in control.

Prayer

Dear God, I know you wish me to be happy and full of hope and not fear. Help me to let go of my fears and to live as a peaceful person. Help me to be a positive example for others. Thank you for giving me courage and insight to let go of what is keeping my energy level down. Help me to recognize how my actions will promote peaceful energy all around me. I am grateful for your love, help, and guidance. Amen

Journal Reflection

Reflect on any fears that have a hold on you. Picture the angels taking your fears to God. Picture your life without fear and worry. Picture your life of peace and safety. Take time to journal about your hopes and dreams.

Flowers, Trees, Plants, and the Fairy Kingdom

Dearest One,

Let the flowers and trees speak to you. They do, you know. They beautify the earth, and as they do, they remind you of your great beauty. All humans need to be reminded of how beautiful they are inside and out. You, like the flowers, are created in the image and likeness of God, the creator. So how can you not be as beautiful as the flowers and trees that decorate your planet? Magazines, TV, and the Internet show humans a false sense of beauty. We angels, see how you glow with bright, beautiful, radiant colors. It is so beautiful and attractive! There are many facets to each of you. Each facet is like an individual petal on a flower. Each petal reaches for the sunlight. Let your many facets reach for and embrace the light of God.

We ask that you listen to the wind in the trees as their leaves whisper to you. Notice the many colors of green that you see in the grass and leaves of trees. Trees have great strength and wisdom. They bend with the wind and are able to handle great storms. They stand strong and firm. They change with the seasons. What can you learn from the trees and the wind?

Plants and trees bring great beauty and clean the air around you. They freely give medicine, fruit, vegetables, nuts, and other raw materials for your use in your daily lives. Thank God and the plant kingdom for these great gifts. Thank the flowers for their fragrance, and their gifts that invoke love, beauty, and romance into your life.

Nature is a gift for humans to experience. Your body and spirit soar when you take time to enjoy the grass, flowers, trees, and air around you. Your prayers reach heaven faster when you are in nature. Your mind becomes more open and less cluttered when you are in nature. The fresh air and fragrance from plants and flowers bring significant health benefits to your body.

There are beautiful creatures called Fairies. They belong to the angelic kingdom. Their jobs are to tend to all the plants, trees, and flowers. Fairies help us to notice the beauty around us. They help us to stop and smell a rose, hug a tree, and to feel the grass under our feet. Fairies dance among the flowers and soar like butterflies. Fairies bring magic, laughter, and music into your life and in the nature that surrounds you. Let nature, the Fairies, and our loving angelic arms surround you to bring you the answers and prayer fulfillment you desire.

Love and heavenly blessings,
The Angelic Kingdom

Author Note

I have plants of various shades of green in my home. I can hear the messages from God, the angels, and the magical fairies clearly when I am near my plants. The plants in my bedroom help me to sleep better at night. I enjoy walking through a wooded area and being among the beautiful trees and plants. I often walk around a lake near my home where there are many trees and plants. I like to pray as I walk or listen for messages. It is very peaceful, calming, and a great way to exercise.

Action Steps

- Buy some plants to be placed inside and outside of your home. Place your plants where you can see them often and enjoy them. It is important to place one or two plants in bedrooms. Plants not only beautify our homes, but they help us to breathe better and will absorb negative energy. They are living things and will appreciate you talking to them!

- Plant a tree for a deceased loved one. This is a great gift for a memorial, an anniversary, or a birthday.
- Buy some fresh flowers for your home. It will brighten your home and your mood.

Affirmation

I am grateful for the beauty of nature around me and for the healing benefits it provides.

Prayer

Dear God, thank you for the beauty of nature that surrounds me. Thank you, angels and fairies, for taking care of the plants, trees, and flowers that beautify our earth. Thank you for the many gifts we receive from nature. Amen

Journal Reflection

1. Sit outside and journal whatever thoughts come to mind. Feel the wind on your face. Feel the sunshine warm you. Look at the trees and plants around you. Thank them for the love they send you.

2. Spend some time going for a walk around your neighborhood, a park, or on a trail. Journal how the experience uplifted you. What prayers or affirmations did you say?

Forgiveness

Dearest One,

　We angels, see many of you carrying around a heavy burden. It is like a stone around your neck. You may not even notice it day to day, because it has become a part of you. For some of you, you have been carrying this burden for years. It is time to forgive. We are not asking you to forgive the action or actions taken against you, but we are asking you to forgive the person or persons who hurt you. We know that forgiving others is not an easy task. We want to remind you that everyone is a child of God, and everyone is doing the best they can at every moment. Forgiving others is allowing yourself to be free. You may forgive someone face to face or maybe you forgive someone in your heart. The other person may not even know you have forgiven them. The act of forgiving acknowledges that you have the courage to rise above the hurt and to live in peace and happiness.

　As you forgive others, we also ask you to forgive someone very special, yourself. Many times, you may believe you caused the hurt or brought upon the anger imposed by others upon you. You may have also hurt others by your words or actions.

　At times, painful memories pop up in your mind. Do not ignore these memories. Realize they are popping up for a reason. These memories wish to be released. Look at the memories and then forgive yourself and those who have hurt you. Once you have forgiven everyone involved, the memory is now released and need not burden you any longer. This may take a while, but each time you forgive, it becomes easier and easier. The feeling of peace and the lightness of the burden being lifted will not only benefit you but the whole planet as well.

Love and heavenly blessings,
The Angelic Kingdom

Author Note

Forgiveness is one of the most important lessons we as humans can learn. Sometimes it is easy to forgive. Sometimes, forgiveness feels like moving a heavy mountain. It seems that the hardest one often to forgive is ourselves. We feel guilty or ashamed. We taunt ourselves with what we did or didn't do.

I grew up Catholic, and some of my friends of other faiths would ask me why Catholics feel they need to go to confession. We believe God forgives us. Why don't we just talk to God? It was a good question and one I also pondered. One Sunday at Mass, my parish priest brought up the subject of confession and forgiveness. He said, "Going to confession brings God's blessings to you. It isn't because God needs to forgive us. He already has. It is because you need to forgive yourself." Truer words have never been spoken. Forgiving ourselves and others will set us free.

Ho'oponopono (ho-o-pono-pono) is a Hawaiian practice of reconciliation and forgiveness. It is a practice I use, and I find it very healing and powerful. The method uses four loving statements.

I am sorry.
Please forgive me.
Thank you.
I love you.

I also like to add two other statements.
Thank you for all you have taught me.
Thank you for all that I have taught you.

I like to picture the person I wish to forgive (including myself) and use this practice. This practice has healed many painful experiences in my life and brought me great peace.

Action Steps

Spend some time alone and picture someone or yourself that needs to be forgiven. Use the phrases from Ho'oponopono to forgive. Permit yourself to cry if needed. Crying helps us release the hurt and the memories associated with the hurt. It is a very powerful process. Depending on the person or situation that needs healing, this may take one or several sessions. Be patient with yourself. Surround yourself with God and your angels. You may want to journal what you feel and experience.

I also encourage you to search Ho'oponopono on the Internet for more information and books that are truly inspiring, and document how miracles have happened using this beautiful and ancient tradition.

Affirmation

I am willing to forgive myself and others. I am truly free.

Prayer

Dear God, I know you have forgiven me for everything I have thought, said, or did, that was not of love for myself or others. Help me to forgive myself and those who have hurt me by words or actions. I know you surround me with love and peace. I know you will help me to forgive so I can feel truly free. Thank you for your help and guidance. Amen

Journal Reflection

1. Reflect on anyone or anything that needs forgiveness in your life.

   Journal about those hurts. When we write about our hurts, it helps release them from our hearts and mind.

2. Journal how you can forgive yourself for any actions, words, or thoughts that have caused others or your self- pain. Use the Ho'oponopono prayer each morning to release, forgive, and bring peace to you and those around you.

Frustration

Dearest One,

Some people will say that life is full of ups and downs. Do you concentrate on only the downs in life and forget about the many ups that have brought you joy and lovely memories? Your path may indeed have times of joy and times of struggle. However, it is through all kinds of experiences that you learn, grow, and evolve into the person you are meant to be.

When you are frustrated, do you ask for help? Do you try to handle it all on your own and are miserable at the same time? God and the angels are here for you and will help you through the good and the bad times. Call on us to help you work through the frustration and to change your perspective on what is frustrating you. We ask that you try and step back from the situation or person that seems to be the cause of your frustration. As you step back, try to look objectively at what you are feeling and experiencing. Are you really frustrated with another person or with yourself? Is this a time to work on patience? Is there another person involved, and you realize that the person may have taken out their frustration on you, but it has nothing to do with you? Rate your frustration level. Is it worth your time and energy, or can you let it go? What can you do to remain calm and to let God and the angels change your frustration to a more harmonious situation? We know that it is not always an easy task, but with practice, you will find that it can be done and can change your whole outlook. Big and little disappointments and worries can be handled with prayer, faith, and a willingness to let God and the angels take away your burdens in exchange for peace and joy.

Love and heavenly blessings,
The Angelic Kingdom

Author Note

We all have frustrating days and feel like things are not going as well as we would like or had planned. There may have been times when you felt that your prayers had not been heard or answered. God does hear and answers your prayers, but not always in the time or manner in which we think it should happen.

I heard a sermon once where the minister explained three reasons why our prayers are not answered in the ways we expect. The first reason asked us to imagine what life would be like if we instantly always got what we wanted. Obviously, if we got what we wanted. so did everyone else. Would anything surprise you anymore? Would you be grateful for anything? Would it really make you happy? Would there be anything to work for or achieve? If you got everything you wanted right away, how would that change the people around you?

The second reason that prayers are not always answered the way we believe is that we would no longer need faith. Our desire to know, love, and trust in God would no longer be needed. We would weaken our connection to God and to our whole belief system. We would wander aimlessly without a purpose or connection to all that really matters.

God knows what is best for us is the third reason. The minister gave the examples of praying for a new job, and you did not receive it or praying that a particular partner would become your spouse. Later, you realize that the job or the spouse would not have made you happy and that, in fact, you would have been miserable. You might have even thought to thank God for *not* answering your prayers. I know that I have experienced this more than once in my life. God knows what the best answers to our prayers should be and asks you to trust.

I also think that there is a fourth reason to consider it. We may have some work to do on ourselves, and it is not the right time or place for our prayers to be answered. Our prayers may be answered when we are more physically, emotionally, and spiritually ready.

Action Steps

I would like you to take some time to think over the last year, month, or even the past week. What struggles or frustrations did you encounter? Are you still struggling with these experiences or have you moved on and grown? Have you prayed and asked for help with these situations or are you trying to handle it all on your own?

Affirmation

I am grateful for the joys and sorrows in my life. I am learning and growing each day. I am supported every step I take.

Prayer

Dear God, I know the importance of prayer. I know you hear my prayers and will answer them in ways I cannot even imagine. Thank you for listening to me. Amen

Journal and Reflection

Journal and reflect on what prayers have been answered and which prayers have not. Take some time to think about why you believe they have not been answered. Have you noticed any blessings in disguise?

Hope

Dearest One,

No matter what the darkest hour seems to be, there is always hope. If hope did not exist, your world would have ended long ago. Hope is a virtue that gives you purpose and the drive to carry on. Hope brings light in what seems to be darkness and despair. Hope helps you face each day and realize that you can and will survive any turmoil you are facing. Hope changes negative thoughts and energy to a more productive and positive energy.

God gives you the gift of hope to reveal "His presence" to you. God is light. He is hope. In the midst of hope, He is whispering to you. Listen to him. Pray to him. He is waiting patiently for you with open arms. We angels are also with you, and we bring you hope and peace. Feel our loving energy around you. Embrace this energy and let it become a part of you.

Love and heavenly blessings,
The Angelic Kingdom

Author Note

The day I wrote this piece was a day filled with signs for me. I had been struggling with some personal challenges and what to do to overcome them. I felt the need to go for a walk. The place I like to visit is beautiful. It has small lakes, trees, flowers, a walking trail, and many benches. I had only walked a short distance when I was told to sit on one of the benches. I was not tired and didn't feel like I needed to sit. However, I have learned not to ignore these messages. When I sat down, I immediately noticed a rock on the bench. The rock was painted beautifully, and the rock had the word "hope" painted on it. It was just what I needed to bring a smile to my face and a jolt to my heart. My energy was lifted, and I knew I was surrounded by my divine team. I walked some more and then sat at a picnic table to write and to talk to God. I also had many butterflies swarming around me. It was a truly wonderful experience!

Action Steps

Think of the word hope. What does it mean to you? What feelings does it bring up? When we feel we are in our deepest hours, the angels and God are even closer to us than we can imagine. Yet, these times also can teach us the greatest lessons. Hope also brings out the best in people. We hear of neighbors helping neighbors in a time of tragedy. People have donated to victims of floods, earthquakes, and hurricanes. How can you be a symbol of hope to others? How have others been a symbol of hope to you? I like to think of hope as:

> **H**eart
> **O**pen
> **P**ositive
> **E**nergy

Talk to God and listen to him. He hears your prayers.

Affirmation

I am filled with hope, for God and the angels, bring new opportunities into my life.

Prayer

Dear God, may today be filled with hope and positive energy. Help pull me out of my struggles and help me to see all of your blessings and gifts around me. Help me to remember that hope never dies. Thank you. Amen

Journal and Reflection

Reflect on this today. Take some time to think of how hope has guided you. Journal what you are most hopeful for at this time in your life. What steps can you take to make your dreams and hopes a reality?

Inspiration

Dearest One,

Inspiration is a gift from God. God is whispering ideas and guidance to you every day. Do you listen to these ideas? Inspiration guides you to make healthy steps to improve all areas of your life. Think of a time when you had a great idea. How did it make you feel? Did it inspire you or others? Did you begin a new project, create something new, or finish an essay? Ask God and the angels for help and inspiration on whatever ideas or projects you wish to create. We are happy to help. God wishes to co-create with you.

Inspiration has created books, plays, scientific discoveries, great art, games, and countless organizations. It does not matter whether the inspirational idea you desire is big or small. It will bring worthwhile changes for you and others. It is a gift that keeps on giving. Listen to the divine idea. Act upon the divine idea. Give thanks for the divine idea. Once you do these things, you will begin to notice more divine ideas coming to you. God's inspirational ideas for you are a never-ending flow of love and abundance.

Love and heavenly blessings,
The Angelic Kingdom

Author Note

My friend and I attended a conference of like-minded individuals. How good it feels to be around people who understand what it means to experience angels, energy work, and spiritual concepts. I knew I was to write this book, yet I was procrastinating. I kept thinking what can I say that others haven't said before? Who wants to hear my words and thoughts? One of the lectures I attended was by a new author. I felt like he was speaking right to me. He reminded me that I had a purpose for writing this book. My voice needed to be heard. He pointed out that my words will help guide others. He encouraged me to think of writing as a service to others. I knew that God was speaking through the author right to my soul. It was a truly joyful weekend. My heart was full of new ideas, confidence, and inspiration. A weekend away can bring joy and rejuvenation to your body and soul.

Action Steps

Inspiration can come from many places. You may read a good book, watch a documentary, listen to a lecture, hear a good sermon, or hear a suggestion from a friend or co-worker. God works through angels and other people to bring inspirational ideas and messages to us. The key is to listen and remember that there are no coincidences. A good rule of thumb to remember is if you hear something three times or more it is a message for you. Write it down. Reflect on it. Pray on it. God is speaking to you. The next step is to take action on the idea and thank God for guiding you.

Affirmation

I am open to new ideas and inspiration from God. I am creative and passionate.

Prayer

Dear God, I ask you to give me clear guidance and inspiration. Please help me to hear your voice and to act upon your divine ideas for me. Thank you for your love, help, and guidance. Amen

Journal Reflection

Who inspires you? What resources inspire you? Is there anything you have ever dreamed of doing? Have you ever felt like you were blocked or "stuck" and need some inspiration? Spend some time journaling your thoughts, ideas, and prayers.

Joy

Dearest One,

We angels are very joyful beings! Why shouldn't we be? God created us, and we joyfully serve God. We each have special missions that involve serving God and the people he created as his own. It brings us great joy to help you and your loved ones in any way we can. Just ask!

We wish you to be joyful as well. God created you to not only to have life but to enjoy your life. We know that you have responsibilities and that some days you will feel sadness or frustration. However, you can find joy every day when you take the time to look for it! When you begin to notice joy and are grateful for it, more joy will come to you. Joy attracts more joy! Isn't that a wonderful thing? Joy can be found in small and large moments of your day. Small moments may include a smile from a stranger that brightens your day or the sound of a child laughing that makes you laugh as well. A friend calls you, and his voice calms you and brings you happiness.

Ask the angels to bring more joy in your life. We are happy to do so. We are happy to help you notice the many joyful moments in your life and to appreciate them. We will also nudge you to bring joy to others. When you choose to give joy to others, you are acting as an earth angel. Notice how your mood and life changes as you begin to add more joy in your life and the life of others. God's abundant universe will respond in kind and will bring even more joy into your life. Begin today and know that your joyful angels surround your joyful experiences!

Love and heavenly blessings,
The Angelic Kingdom

Author Note

Think of the word enjoy. The word joy is in it! Do you enjoy your life and the people in it? Do you enjoy your work and your play? These are important questions to ponder. I do enjoy my work and spending time with friends and family. I feel very blessed to have a good life, and I am truly grateful. Yet, at times I admit I need to stop and reflect on the joyful moments that I am experiencing. I have had to make a conscious effort to look for joy when I felt like my life was not always going the way I wanted or planned. Living in the present moment and finding joy is not always easy to do. It is hard to find joy at times when we are faced with difficulties or hardships. Yet, joy is still waiting to be found. It is God reminding you that he is with you in every moment. He is there in good and bad times.

It is easy to believe that joy is in the future. I will be happier when I am at a new job. I will be joyful when I meet my soulmate. Joy is for those who have more money than I do. We all have the power to experience joy at this very moment. Joy wants to be felt and experienced. Joy wants to be discovered and acknowledged. Did you know that some angels are named Joy? I encourage you to feel joy right now. The more you realize the joyful moments in your day, the more joy will come to you.

Action Steps

Here are some ways to try and bring more joy into your life. Joy is a gift for all people. Joy is found in even the darkest situations. You do not have to look hard for it. It is there. You can always call on the angels to bring more joy into your life.

- Set the timer on your watch or phone for three hours. When the timer goes off, take a few minutes for reflection. What happened in that short amount of time that made you happy or made you smile? Did a coworker smile at you? Did someone compliment you? Did your child hug you this morning? Did someone hold the door for you? These little things mean a lot. Notice them, and thank God for them, and more moments will be brought to you.

- Look at old photographs. What memories bring you joy? What stories do they help you recall?
- Think about one way you can bring joy to someone's day today. Is there someone you can smile at on your way to work? Is there someone you know that needs someone to listen to them? Remember, you may be the angel they need that day!
- When you need a boost on a particularly sad or rough day, you can choose to bring joy into your day. You can dispel your sadness or anger by reading a joke, watching a funny movie or TV show, reading an inspirational quote, coloring a picture, or reading a good book. These suggestions will not only help change your mood and your day, but will elevate your energy.

Affirmation

I am able to see the joy in my life. I enjoy life to the fullest.

Prayer

Dear God, I thank you for the gift of joy in my life. I know that you wish me to enjoy my life and to help spread joy to others by my words and actions. I ask that the angels surround me with joy so we can work together to make our world a joyful place to be. Amen

Journal Reflection

Spend time thinking about your day or the past week. What moments made you laugh or to feel joy? What are things you enjoy doing? Journal how you can bring more joy into your life. How can you bring joy to the life of other people?

Life Lessons

Dearest One,

Did you know that part of our mission as angels, and part of your mission is to allow us to work with you, around you, and within you? It is a mission we do not take lightly. It is a mission we are happy to fulfill. We wish you to live a happy, loving, and light-filled life. We are here to help you in all aspects of your physical and spiritual life. You have come to earth to learn lessons and to help you grow spiritually. That is not to say that you will not have ups and downs in your life. The ups and downs that you feel are opportunities for growth and lessons to be learned. As humans, you can decide if you want to fully absorb the lesson provided the first time or to experience the lesson many times to master it. You will also have the freedom to decide how your reaction to each lesson will be. As your angels, we can and will guide you through each lesson and opportunity in a gentle way. Once learned, it may not have to be presented to you again.

However, if the opportunity is not addressed or learned, the situation will keep presenting itself over and over again until you deal with it. You will find some lessons a joy to discover. You will find that some lessons may cause your heart to break, or you may have to face some fears that you have.

Be aware as well, that some lessons may run very deep inside of you. You may work on layer after layer until the lesson is learned. Through it all, God and the angels will fully support you and guide you. You need to ask us, and it is done. You are never alone on your journey. Each lesson or experience enables you to grow closer to God and to truly live and grow as a child of God.

Love and heavenly blessings,
The Angelic Kingdom

Author Note

I have experienced lessons and opportunities for growth many times in my life. Some lessons, like a car accident, may only be needed to be experienced once. Often there are lessons for both drivers to learn. Financial lessons have taken me many lessons and opportunities to learn. However, finding my soulmate has been one of the hardest growth experiences I have had to face. It has been a process of learning for many years. The process has involved experiencing and peeling back layers after layers of work to be done on myself, and to examine the dating choices I have made. I know that each relationship I have experienced has taught me valuable lessons, and I have also taught others through these experiences. This process has not been easy, and it has often been very painful. I know that my angels have been there through every joy and heartbreak. They have supported me and encouraged me to find out who I truly am and to truly love myself.

Action Steps

When faced with a situation or situations that seem to be difficult to handle or takes you out of your comfort zone, remember that this is an opportunity for growth. These life lessons teach and prepare you for new and greater opportunities. The first thing to do is to realize that all situations are lovingly supported by God and the angels. You are never alone. The second thing to understand is that not every lesson is negative or needs to be perceived in a negative way. If you are saying to yourself, "why me," then it is time to switch your way of thinking to "why not me?" Ask yourself what can I gain from this experience? What can I learn? Can I turn this negative situation into an opportunity for growth? Did I meet someone because of this opportunity? Pray and ask for guidance and assistance. Pray and ask for strength to face the difficult situations you encounter. Pray and give thanks for the joyful experiences that God brings you. God will always bring you opportunities that help you to grow. God will only bring you opportunities that he knows you are able to handle. You are always in the hands of God. Enjoy the journey!

Affirmation

I am learning, growing, and experiencing all that life has to offer.

Prayer

Dear God, I know that you are with me on every step of my journey through life. I ask you to help me see your loving hand in every joyful and sorrowful experience you bring me. I ask you to help me to not only learn the lessons presented but also to recognize the growth I am making and to be patient with myself through the process. Each day, I can grow, change, and live my journey in peace and happiness. Amen

Journal Reflection

What life lessons have been very difficult for you? How did you make it through the hard times? What life lessons have been very joyful for you? Who has been there with you on your journey?

Life Purpose

Dearest One,

At times we hear people ask what is my life purpose? What does God want me to do with my life? How can I serve others? I feel like I am meant for something else, but what is it? These are all good questions, and we applaud you for reflecting on them. Your soul speaks to you and guides you to fulfill your special mission on earth. Yes, every one of you does have a special mission. You have come to earth to learn and to grow. Every experience you have or every person you interact with is an opportunity for growth and expansion. There are people you teach and others that teach you. Have you noticed that some people come into your life for just a short time and others for a lifetime? You are always learning and growing. Change will always happen. You may or may not change jobs in your lifetime. You may or may not marry. You may go to college or right to the workforce. You may experience the miracle of birth or the death of a loved one. Each experience helps you grow as a soul. Each profession teaches you skills and lessons. A waitress learns customer service, patience, balance, and a desire to serve others. A farmer learns about animals, crops, soil, and the weather. A mechanic learns how to work with their hands, how to listen to sounds, how to diagnose problems, and how to fix the problems. A parent learns patience and understanding. A student learns academic as well as life skills. The occupation you are in is part of your life purpose

When you are questioning, what is my life purpose? You are listening to your inner guidance. You are ready for something new. It may be time for a new job or career. It may be time to go back to school. It may be time for a new relationship with a new friend, a new romantic partner, or a new relationship with yourself. It may be time to begin learning a new creative hobby that brings you great pleasure. Your life purpose may be leading you to a more spiritual path of learning.

Whatever you are feeling is an indicator of what your soul is longing to experience. Follow your heart and your intuition to the next part of your journey, taking with you the lessons you have already learned. What is your life purpose?

- Your purpose is to live each day to the fullest.
- Learn something new each day.
- Live each day without a single regret.
- Live each day, helping at least one other person.
- Live each day in peace and happiness.
- Love yourself and others.

Love and heavenly blessings,
The Angelic Kingdom

Author Note

Several years ago, a good friend and I attended a spiritual conference. It was a conference of like-minded individuals. How good it felt to be around people who understood what it meant to experience angels, energy work, and spiritual concepts. It was truly a joyful weekend. My heart was full of new ideas and inspirations. It was a weekend that reviewed concepts previously learned and a chance to learn new insights and concepts. It was a beautiful way to enjoy and feel a group consciousness filled with light, love, and high vibrational energy.

How joyful we feel when we are doing what we love to do and are called to do. I was blessed to know right out of high school that I was to be an elementary teacher, and that was my calling. It was a rewarding profession for over thirty-four years. It was also a wonderful experience that taught me many lessons. Around my thirty-second year of teaching I realized that I was being called to move into another profession. I had been working part-time as a healer and an angel reader, but it was time to become a full-time healer, angel reader, and author. It did not happen overnight. It took another two years before I was completely ready to make a transition. However, as I began to make this transition, I realized that teaching was a precursor for my next phase in my life. It taught me how to write, how to speak in front of groups, how to teach all subjects and ages, how to listen to others, and, most importantly, how to serve others. God's plan for me was there all along. I was and am serving my life purpose. My life purpose will continue to grow and change, and I will grow and change with it.

The angels have told me that we have many paths to choose from. Some paths are easier to follow than others. However, the wonderful thing is that each path leads to the same destination. Choose the path that is right for you at this moment in your life and know that it will lead you to your correct destination.

Action Steps

If you are wondering if you are following your life purpose, take some time to stop and reflect on what makes you happy. What do you like about your current job or career? What doesn't make you happy? Who are the people in your life currently that are allowing you to grow and change? Of course, we need to realize all jobs will have aspects we like or do not like. There are people in our lives that we enjoy being around and some who try our patience. However, when we realize that this job or these people in our lives are currently preparing us for the next leg of our journey, we can appreciate the lessons and experiences that have helped us to grow into the person we are.

When you take some time to reflect and write down your thoughts, you begin to create a new step on your journey. You begin to recognize new opportunities or people that are coming into your life. When you are clearer as to what you would like to bring into your life, God and the universe will answer.

Affirmation

I am living my life purpose with love, light, and learning.

Prayer

Dear God, I am ready to embrace the new in my life, and I thank you for the life lessons of the old. Help me to let go of what is ready to go and to allow the new to come in. Amen

Journal Reflection

1. After you have reflected on what makes you happy, take some time to journal on what else would make you happy or feel fulfilled. What is something you have always wanted to do? What is something you have always wanted to learn?

2. What are some steps you can take right now to help you achieve a goal or begin a new path?

3. Is there a class, job, or career that seems to get your attention? Take some time to explore the internet or network with people who are involved in the areas you are interested in.

4. Challenge yourself to try something new each week or once a month. It is amazing how the energy changes you. You will be more open to opportunities and more confident in yourself.

Listen to Your Body

Dearest One,

Do you realize that your body talks to you in amazing ways? You may notice some messages already. You know that when your stomach growls, you know you are hungry. You yawn and know that your body is ready to rest and sleep. Your body is truly a remarkable creation, and all your organs, cells, and systems work together so you can live your life to the fullest.

It is important to listen to your body and follow the advice it is giving you. Your muscles ask you to exercise them and to massage them often. Your muscles know that regular exercise will keep you feeling strong and balanced throughout your day. It is also essential to stretch your muscles each morning, and before and after exercise. Your muscles will also speak to you when you have overworked them, and you need to rest them.

Your bones ask you to stay strong and stand tall. Your bones may creak when they want you to give them some attention. Pay attention to how you work on your computer or devices. Are you crouching? How are you bending?

Your brain craves knowledge and urges you to learn something new each day. Reading new information and connecting it to previous knowledge will build your memory and brain cells. Working on puzzles, math problems, and games will also keep your brain happy and healthy.

When you feel sick, it is your body telling you to slow down, rest, and get back to what is most important.

The angels ask you to be more aware and conscious of your body, and all it does for you. Thank your body every day, and your body will reward you with love, strength, and good health.

Love and heavenly blessings,
The Angelic Kingdom

Author Note

I have noticed that in the last few years, my body is becoming more sensitive to jewelry, lotions, perfumes, and chemicals. I have also noticed that if I am lying on a pillow in the wrong position, I hear little squeaks from my head and neck. The first time I heard this noise, I thought it sounded like a little voice. I wasn't sure what it was. After hearing it several times, I realized it was my body telling me that my position on the pillow was not good for me. I moved my head and neck, adjusted my pillow, and listened. I did not hear the sound anymore.

I also have learned to talk to my body. I will admit I need to work on this every day. I do not always remember to do this. However, when I do, it is amazing how much better I feel. Several years ago, my knees were hurting. I made a concentrated effort to massage my knees every night, and I would say to them that I appreciated them. I thanked my knees for holding me up and helping me move and bend throughout the day. After about three weeks, my knees felt amazing!

Archangel Michael also told me to talk to my body and appreciate how beautiful I am and how beautiful my body is. I like to put lotion on after a shower or bath. As I put the lotion on, I thank my arms, legs, and other body parts for all they do for me throughout the day. It is incredible how your body reacts. You feel stronger, happier, healthier, and more beautiful!

Action Steps

- Listen to your body. If you react to a particular lotion, soap, or perfume, stop using it right away. Your body is intelligent and knows what is best for you.
- If you are feeling antsy, your body is telling you it is time to move. Get up and go for a walk. Your mind and body will appreciate it!
- Talk to your body. Thank your body for all it is doing for you. If possible, gently touch or massage your body as you

thank each of your vital parts. You can use the suggestions I have listed or make up your own.

1. Thank you, arms, for helping me hold things, to hug my child, to carry groceries, to drive my car, and to lift the laundry basket each day.

2. Thank you, legs, for helping me walk today, for holding me up, and for helping me be mobile all day long.

3. Thank you, feet, for holding me and keeping me balanced.

4. Thank you, hands and fingers for helping me type, text, and to grasp things.

5. Thank you, all my vital organs, for helping me to live and to be happy and healthy each day.

6. Thank you brain, for helping me to think, problem-solve, and to learn. Thank you, brain, for helping all of my organs and body parts to work well together.

7. Thank you, my heart, for pumping blood through my entire body and for helping me to love and to be loved.

Affirmation

I am strong, healthy, happy, and young!

Prayer

Dear God, thank you, for my beautiful and miraculous body that you have created for me. Help me to take care of it and to appreciate all it does for me each day. Amen

Journal Reflection

Write a letter to your body. Thank your body for all that it does for you. What are some good habits you do for your body? What are some habits you would like to change?

Love Is All There Is

Dearest One,

Love is all there is. Love creates. Love conquers all. Love solves conflicts. Love is powerful. Love unites us. Love makes life worth living. Love is all around us. God is love. You may have heard or have said many of these statements. There is nothing more powerful or stronger than love. Without love, your world would feel lifeless, lonely, and powerless. Yet, you are never without love. Love surrounds you. It engulfs you. It is you! God is love, and he created you in love. He surrounds you and all inhabitants of the earth in love. God is love, and you are one with God so you can never escape love. There are many kinds of love, but all love comes from God.

Angels surround you daily with love and light. You cannot escape it. Why would you want to? It is given freely. We ask that you open your heart to accept this great love. Let our help and love transform your lives. There is nothing more transforming than love. Love is what makes your world go around.

Love and heavenly blessings,
The Angelic Kingdom

Author Note

One of my favorite movies of all time is "Love Actually." The film touches upon many facets of love and how the characters are changed by love. Our lives are not a movie, however, many of us can relate to some of the situations in the movie. The film is a comedy, yet it also speaks too sad moments in our lives, like death, betrayal, and heartache. As in the film, I have experienced many of the same situations of falling in love, heartache, losing a loved one, and the love I receive from my family. When I look at my life, I know God has, is and will be, with me through it all. The angels are also with me, bringing me new people in my life to love and to be loved by.

I was very blessed to have grown up in a loving family. I knew I was loved and I loved my parents and seven siblings very much. When I went off to college, I realized that we didn't speak the words "I love you" very often. I decided to change that. Whenever, I came home from college or called my parents, I always ended the conversation with "I love you." As adults, my siblings and my parents, now always end our conversations and gatherings saying those words. We have taught our nieces and nephews to do the same. Three little words that mean more than anything else in the world.

Action Steps

- Tell three people this week how much you love them.
- Donate items to a homeless shelter. Ask that love surround your donations so that the person receiving the items feel the love.
- Ask your angels to surround you and your family and friends with love.
- Ask that love be sent to all people in the world.
- Hold your hands over your heart. Send love to your heart and your whole body. Thank your heart for the love and life it brings to you daily.

Affirmation

I am loved. I am lovable. I radiate love to others.

Prayer

Dear God, thank you for loving me and surrounding me with love. I ask that you only bring loving situations into my life. Help me to receive your love with open arms. Help me to love others and to give my love freely. Amen

Journal Reflection

Think back on your life and reflect on the types of love you have given and have received. What memories does it bring up?

How can you show your love to others? How has your love transformed someone else? Whose love is transforming you?

Loving Yourself

Dearest One,

There are many kinds of love, but the greatest love of all is loving yourself. You are truly God's child. Yet, many of you feel inadequate or feel that others are somehow better than you. Some of you feel unworthy of love because of what you may have or have not done in the past. Some people feel that their physical appearance or personality keeps them from love. The material world teaches you to wear this outfit, change this habit, act, or look a certain way, and you will be attractive to others. When you finally make all these changes, then you will love yourself more and others will love you.

Nothing could be further from the truth! You are perfect in every way. You are a child of God. How could you be anything less? As good parents love their children unconditionally, so does your loving Father in heaven. He knows your struggles, your pains, your failures, and the many successes you have experienced. His love for you never wavers. His great love and light burn in you every day. Nothing you say or do can take you from his love. Nothing you can say or do can take the angels away from you. You are pure light and true love. When you love yourself, you are able to give and receive all kinds of love. People are drawn to you not because of how you look or what you wear, but who you truly are. When you love yourself, your light burns even brighter! Your aura is pink and sparkly! We angels are not saying that you should never improve yourself, or break unhealthy habits, but we are saying that you should begin loving yourself right now! Do not wait until you have become a perfect person in your eyes or the eyes of others. You are perfect in God's eyes. Love yourself and watch the miracles around you appear!

Love and heavenly blessings,
The Angelic Kingdom

Author Note

Loving myself has been a lifelong lesson. At an early age, we are bombarded with media and people showing us images of what we should or shouldn't be. We are also told that loving yourself is selfish. It is selfish to do things for yourself. You should think of others first then yourself. Vanity is a sin. We may also have had people tell us that we should lose weight, or change our hairstyle, or change the way we walk or talk. Did these suggestions help you or hinder you? Did they make you feel inferior? Did you feel unlovable? I know I felt that way at times. These messages can be ingrained in us and hard to change. However, with practice, they can be changed. The angels told me to tell myself every day that I was lovable and that I loved myself. They encouraged me to make healthy choices. They reminded me that loving myself would teach others to do the same. Loving myself would not only increase my self-esteem, but would increase my time, energy, and finances. The angels encouraged me to talk to myself in the mirror each day and to tell myself I was beautiful and lovable. I was told to do this several times a day. The angels asked me to tell my image and myself, "I love you."

I have found that most women have a very hard time looking in the mirror and saying they love themselves. It is not always easy, and it can be somewhat uncomfortable at times. Yet, I persisted, and I began to see results. I felt stronger, happier, and more confident! After working on this action step for several weeks, I began telling myself that I looked beautiful and younger each day. I did that as often as I could during the day. A few weeks later, I was scheduled to have lunch with two friends. I had not seen these friends for over two years. They are cute, slim women. I arrived at the restaurant and immediately saw one of my friends. She greeted me with a hug and then began to tell me that I looked beautiful. I was taken aback. This was not something that we usually said to each other. I thanked her, and we began talking about our lives. My second friend arrived later on and hugged me. Then she told me that I looked beautiful.

I was close to tears. I was not expecting this to happen. As my two friends were chatting, I heard Archangel Michael say to me, "Did you hear what they said to you?" It was so powerful and up-lifting. It changed my life.

Action Steps

When we are happy, loving, and have a positive outlook, the universe responds in kind. We will notice that opportunities come our way, finances improve, relationships improve, and we are less stressed. When we love ourselves, and treat ourselves, we can give more to others. Use action steps today to begin to love yourself and your body. Your mind and body will hear you. The universe hears you. Watch the miracles appear in your life. You will never be the same.

- Begin by telling yourself that you love yourself.
- Talk to yourself in the mirror. Look at yourself and thank yourself for all that you are and for all that you do. Tell yourself you are beautiful or handsome. Tell yourself that you look younger and feel younger. You are energized and healed. Whatever words you use make them positive and powerful. Notice what happens in the next weeks to come!

Affirmation

I am lovable. I am loved. I am worthy of great love.

Prayer

Dear God, I am thankful that you have created me in a lovingly and perfectly. You see me as I truly am. Help me to see me as I truly am. I am lovable and worthy of great love. Amen

Journal Reflection

1. Reflect on your self-image. How do you see yourself? Journal the things you like and love about yourself.

2. Reflect and journal on ways you can love yourself more.

3. Spend time talking to yourself in the mirror. Reflect and journal on what happens after doing this for several weeks.

Mind Clutter

Dearest One,

Clutter seems to be increasing in your world. Many thoughts or possessions clutter and fill up your mind. Often, we hear humans complain about the clutter and want to clear it out. However, humans have no idea how to begin. First, we ask that you call on us for help. Secondly, we ask that you remember that decluttering can be done. Thirdly, we ask that you be kind to yourself and forgive yourself for the clutter.

We want to start with the clutter in your mind. Your mind is filled with many thoughts each day. Thoughts about your family, job, home, finances, and the world keep your mind cluttered and overwhelmed. There are some suggestions we offer for you to bring you peace and happiness.

- Begin each day talking to God. Spending some alone time with God, even a few minutes, will reap many rewards.

- Ask God and the angels to help you with all you must do and think about that day. We are glad to help, and you will notice your burdens becoming lighter.

- We encourage you to limit TV and screen time on your devices. These electronic devices can clutter your mind with many unnecessary thoughts and worries.

- Limit the number of negative TV programs you watch. These programs can fill your mind with negative thoughts, worries, and fears.

- Read something inspirational each day. Inspirational books, calendars, cards, and podcasts will build your relationship with God and others and fill your thoughts with positive messages.

Love and heavenly blessings,
The Angelic Kingdom

Author Note

It has been my experience that I do not think as clearly if there is clutter around me. My energy level drops when I have too many items out of place in my home or at work. I have found that I can hear God and the angel's messages when my mind and home are clear of messes and distractions. I find decluttering a necessary and healthy way to live. Often, I help friends and family to declutter. I want to offer you some practical ways to declutter that are helpful and proven energy boosters.

- Talk to God and the angels daily. Ask for their help and listen for any messages and guidance they have for you that day.

- Limit your phone and TV time each day. I find I have more time in my day and get more accomplished when I do this.

- Read an inspirational quote each day from an app or a website. Buy a daily calendar that has positive quotes, messages, and affirmations.

- One day a month, sit down and go through your bills for the month and list them in your check register. I have set up automatic payment for most of my bills. I go through receipts I have collected. I file those I need and shred those I don't need.

- When it is tax time, go through all your saved files and shred any you no longer need. I only have one file box. This helps me find things quickly, and there are not stacks of papers around that can clutter my mind and my home.

- Weekly, trash, or unsubscribe to any emails that you no longer need. It will save you time and energy each day. If there are emails you need to keep, put them in files provided by your email provider. You can find them quickly, and will find that seeing twenty-five to fifty emails instead of one hundred emails, will decrease your stress level immediately. Don't forget to empty the trash and the scam files on your computer. This small gesture will boost energy levels and will remove unwanted negativity.

- Clear out your phone's text messages and phone logs weekly to free up space and clutter.

I encourage you to try one or more of these suggestions. Notice how much healthier and more balanced; you begin to think and feel.

Action Steps

Choose one of the listed activities and work on it until it becomes a habit. Then gradually, add another activity to your lifestyle. You will soon find that the other activities or suggestions will become easier and will help lower your clutter and stress.

Purchase an inspirational calendar, app, or book. Read it as you are getting ready in the morning. This habit will bring more joy and purpose to your day.

Affirmation

I am to think clearly. My mind is free from clutter and distractions that do not serve me.

Prayer

Dear God, I ask you to help me declutter my mind, so that I can hear your guidance and help. I know that decluttering can increase my productivity and wellness. Thank you for your support. Amen

Journal Reflection

Take some time to reflect on your busy day. What thoughts clutter your mind with worry, stress, or negativity? What thoughts bring you joy and happiness? Journal on one way you can declutter today. When you have used several methods of decluttering, reflect, and journal on how your mind and body feel.

Miracles

Dearest One,

Many of you think that miracles are uncommon. You believe that miracles are something you have heard or read about, but you could never experience it. The truth is that miracles are happening all around you and for you, all the time. The more you notice them and are grateful for them, the more you receive. God's love is always expanding, and his gifts for you expand as well. When you believe and accept the miracles in your life, it not only benefits you, but it benefits those you love. The fact is there are no coincidences. Everything happens for a reason and is part of God's divine plan for you and your purpose. When you pray and ask for help, God and the angels begin to work on your behalf. Your job is to ask and to trust that your prayers will be answered in miraculous ways. When you start to notice that God is with you every step of the way, you will see miracles happening in your life and the lives of those around you.

Big miracles are occurring all the time. The sun rises and sets each day. The seasons change each year. You hear that someone is cancer- free after a long battle with the disease. You are watching the news and hear that a family is safe after a house fire. A lost dog finds the way home. A child is adopted into a wonderful family. Long lost family members are reunited after a long separation. You are driving, and you miss being hit by another car. You have experienced some of these miracles have you not?

Some miracles will be small but are incredible, just the same! You run into a friend that you haven't seen for a long time. You think about a certain person, and then you receive a phone call from them. You find money in your pants pocket that you swore wasn't there before. You find a lost treasured item that has been missing for several years. You are struggling with a problem, and the right answer suddenly comes to you! There has been something you desire to have but feel you can't afford it, and you receive the exact item from a friend.

Ask for help from God and the angels and then listen and watch for signs of miracles. Thank God for them, and you will find that miracles happen every day! Remember that you are a miracle!

Love and heavenly blessings,
The Angelic Kingdom

Author Note

Since I began asking the angels to be in my life, I have noticed miracles occurring in so many wonderful and unexpected ways! One weekend I was driving out of town to visit my cousin for a fun girl's weekend. My bank account was dipping low, and I was hesitant to leave town. However, I also knew that the angels told me it was time to have some fun. I trusted that the money would come and that I would have a great weekend. I stopped at a convenience store for gas and some snacks. I saw that there was a candy bar on sale. I don't usually purchase a candy bar, but decided it was just what I needed. I went out to my car and put my purse and candy bar on the seat. A few miles down the road, the candy bar slipped under the seat. I could not reach it. I decided someone was telling me I didn't need to eat it. I had a great weekend and left for home. I again stopped at the same gas station to fill up. I remembered the candy bar that had slipped down under the seats. I moved back the seat, and there was my candy bar melted. However, there was also an envelope. I opened it, and there was a check from my insurance company for $150.00! It was also dated and would have expired in ten more days! I was so happy and so grateful!

Another miracle I would like to share with you occurred one day when I left work and went out to my car. The doors were locked. I got in and noticed my seat was pulled all the way back. It looked as if a very tall man had been in my car. I wasn't scared. I knew this had happened for a reason. I turned my car on and tried to adjust my seat. It took over ten minutes to adjust my seat. Then I heard that the angels had prevented me from being hit by another car. If I had left ten minutes sooner, I would have been in an accident. I was so grateful for the protection.

Action Steps

When you hear something wonderful that has happened immediately, thank God for the miracle. Listen when other people say the word miracle in a story they are telling. Review your day and notice the great blessings you encountered throughout the day. How did God or the angels assist you? Did anything happen that shows a God incident, not a coincidence? Ask for and be open to the angels and God bringing miracles into your life

Affirmation

I am open to receiving miracles in my life.

Prayer

Dear God, I thank you for the many miracles in my life and the life of those around me. Help me to notice your hand in helping me on my journey. Amen

Journal Reflection

Do you recall any God incidents in your life? What miracles have you encountered? Journal ways God is working in your life and in the life of those you love.

Patience

Dearest One,

Patience is a virtue. In your fast-paced world, patience is not only a virtue, it is a necessity. Think of how many times you are called upon in a day to be patient.

- waiting in traffic to get to your destination
- waiting in a line for a coffee
- waiting at the checkout counter at a grocery store
- a child demanding your attention
- your boss adds more work to your already full workload

The angels know of your daily tasks and demands. They ask you to call upon them for patience as you go through your busy day. Ask God and the angels for patience as you work with others, with your children, fellow drivers, community members, and, most of all, with yourself. When you call upon the angels for help, your day goes smoother. You will notice that obstacles are removed from your path. You will find that you accomplish more in a shorter amount of time.

The angels know how important it is to get your tasks done yet have time for your family, for fun, and for yourself. Ask your angels to help you each day to be patient with yourself and others and notice the difference in your life.

Love and heavenly blessings,
The Angelic Kingdom

Author Note

Often, I have been told that I have an incredible amount of patience. As a teacher, you naturally need to have patience with your students. However, every teacher will tell you that they can have days when they lose their patience! I can admit that it has happened to me many times. I have also noticed that I can be very patient with some people and situations, and other times, I have very limited patience. When I lack patience, I know it can come across in my face and my voice. Do you ever feel this way? I have found that I become more patient when I recognize what is making me lose patience and why. Are my stress and worries, causing this impatience? Was I running late, and now I am impatient with other drivers or in the checkout line? Is the person in front of me elderly and needs more time? When I stop to see how I am reacting, I can also change that reaction. It usually takes only a few minutes to do, and it can change my mood and my level of patience. It takes practice, but it does work. When I feel that I am becoming impatient, I first stop and take three deep breaths. Deep breathing instantly calms me and centers me. Then I look at the situation objectively as I can. Then I ask God and the angels to bring me peace and patience and to assist the situation. When I ask for help, it is always given. My reaction, my voice control, and my facial expression can change to a much calmer demeanor. It is a good reminder to me that others have been patient with me.

I can be very impatient with myself as well. I want to complete a task accurately and efficiently, and it doesn't always go as planned. Asking for divine help reminds me that I am not alone, and help is always there. When I ask for help and accept it, I accomplish what I need to and with a better outcome than I anticipated.

Action Steps

The next time you are in a situation where you need to be patient, remember to ask God and the angels to keep you calm and peaceful. Practice taking deep breaths and look at the situation from another perspective. When you act with patience and are patient, others notice and will learn from you!

117

Affirmation

I am patient with myself and others.

Prayer

Dear God, help me to be patient with others and with myself. Help me to remember that we are all on a journey of learning. I know that with your love, guidance, and assistance, I can stay centered even in the most stressful situations. Thank you for your help and assistance. Amen

Journal Reflection

Take some time to reflect on what makes you feel impatient or stressed? Have you been impatient this week? In what situations are you most patient? Do you view yourself as a patient person?

Peace

Dearest One,

Peace is what the world needs most; some people will say. I wish my life were more peaceful, others will say. How can I bring peace into my life and the world? How can one person make a difference? With God and the angels on your side, you can have peace in your life and make a difference in the lives of others.

Angels are pure love and light. We can fill you, your home, your workspace, your city, and your country with God's divine love and light. All you need to do is ask, and it is done. Calling on angels enables us to complete our heavenly missions as well as your divine mission. When you call on us for light and peace, you will notice your life and the lives around you changing for the better. We ask that you not only call on us but also practice becoming a person of peace. Sit quietly and breathe deeply. Picture white angel light filling your entire body from the top of your head to the tips of your toes. Breathe deeply. Relax and feel how peaceful your mind and body become.

We encourage you to do this at least once a day, if possible, several times during the day. It is a perfect way to destress and to calm fears and anxiety. Let this become a habit for you. You will be amazed at how calm, patient, and relaxed you will become. You will let irritations slide off you. Your peaceful manner will also influence others to be peaceful and calm.

After sitting in silence, picture your home surrounded by light and peace. Visualize every room of your home enveloped in light and peace. Ask the angels to bring this gift to your workspace, which will be enjoyed by all who work there.

Visualize four angels, one at each corner of your city, state, or country. Visualize the first two angels holding a blanket of white, peaceful light and bringing that beautiful blanket across your city, state, or country. Visualize this beautiful blanket for other countries or cover the whole world.

This process only takes a few minutes, but the results are powerful! You are co-creating with God and the angels, a peaceful environment for all earthly inhabitants. You can and do make a difference!

Love and heavenly blessings,
The Angelic Kingdom

Author Note

This exercise in peace and light came to me one day. I was breathing deeply and centering myself on hearing the angels. I saw four angels on each corner of a country at war. I saw the angels pull white light across the country. It was so beautiful. I was told to picture this white light around situations that I heard about on the news or heard about from others around me. I began picturing white and pink light around countries around the world and in my own country. I was told that it was very powerful and that I was contributing to a peaceful world. I have also used this exercise to cover my work and home environments.

Action steps

Sit quietly for ten minutes: picture white, peaceful light coming down your entire body. Take several deep breaths and remind yourself you are a peaceful person. During your busy day, stop and breathe deeply. Remind yourself of the beautiful peace that is within you.

If you encounter situations or people, who are not at peace, instantly ask the angels to surround the situation or persons with white, peaceful light. Remain calm and grounded in your peace. Do not get caught up in the drama. Your peaceful demeanor will create peace and harmony.

In the morning or at night, picture peaceful light surrounding your neighborhood, city, state, and country. You are a powerful light worker in this way, and your contribution will yield positive benefits.

Affirmation

I am a peaceful person. I am bringing peace to the world.

Prayer

Dear God, help me to be a person of peace. Help me to stay calm and centered in your love. Amen

Journal Reflection

Journal and reflect on the following questions: What does the word "peace" mean to you? Do you feel peaceful? Why or why not? Do you believe that one person can make a difference?

Play

Dearest One,

All work and no play makes for a very long day. Play is essential for all humans of ALL ages! Your TV commercials or fitness experts often suggest living a balanced life. Your angels agree with this as well. Add some form of play into your day to day routine. Play nurtures you and helps you relax. Playtime builds your intellectual and emotional well- being. It is well documented that children learn from play. It is the same for adults as well. The importance of play is not to be ignored. When you take time to play, you increase your productivity, and you generally feel happier. Play does not need to cost a lot of money or even take a lot of time. However, the benefits are worth their weight in gold. Here are some ideas to help you relax, to smile, and to fill your inner child.

- Play with a child.
- Remember a fond memory.
- Call a friend just to chat.
- Read a good book.
- Have dinner out with friends.
- Laugh at a joke.
- Watch a funny TV show or movie.
- Watch home movies or videos.
- Play frisbee, jump rope or walk barefoot in the grass.
- Play a board game.
- Dance or sing to your favorite song!
- Get a massage.
- Draw, paint or, color.
- Play or watch a favorite sport.
- Take a nap outside.
- Go to a concert or a community theater production.

- Go to a lecture or an art gallery opening.
- Go for a hike or ride your bike on a trail.
- Enjoy a concert in the park.

Love and heavenly blessings,
The Angelic Kingdom

Author Note

I often spend time with friends in the pursuit of playtime. We spend time chatting, having lunch, or dinner out, or we meet for a movie. These friendships nurture me and help me to relax, unwind, and enjoy the life God has given me.

Play does not need to involve another person or persons. Spend time alone reading a great book, taking a nap, getting a massage or manicure, or watching a TV show that makes you happy. Pampering yourself is a form of play that brings health benefits for your mind and body.

Action Steps

Think about what brings joy into your life. What activities can you do this week that would bring fun into your life? How does it feel to add these daily doses of fun and playtime to your week? Remember, a fun activity does not need to cost money. Notice how much more balanced you become. Playtime is not an option. It is a balanced way of life. Let your inner child play and see how good life can be!

Affirmation

I am happy with my work and my play.

Prayer

Dear God, help me to bring more play time into my weekly and daily activities. Help me to see the importance of play in my wellbeing. Help me to feel the balance of work and play. I am grateful for the opportunities you bring to me. Amen

Journal Reflection

Think about what ways you add play to your daily life. Do you need to add more playtime?

Procrastination

Dearest One,

How many times do you procrastinate on something you know you should do or are called to do? Somehow, you rationalize why you need to put it off or believe you are not ready to do it. Procrastination often occurs when you think everything has to be perfect or lined up correctly before you can begin. Often, people will put time limits or constraints on themselves or projects. They believe the project or task will take hours or days to do, so they don't want to begin. At times, you procrastinate because you believe you are not the right person or are not qualified for the task. We angels also know that you are hard on yourself or even berate yourself when you don't begin or finish the task. You also know that if you did face the task ahead of you, you would be glad that you did and would realize it wasn't as big of a challenge as you thought it would be.

Procrastination can be a sign of fear. The fear of failure, fear of rejection, fear of the unknown, and even fears of success can lead to procrastination. These are ego-based fears based on false evidence appearing real. When you are faced with a task, ask the angels to help you with it. Ask your ego to step aside and begin to dive in. You will be relieved to have started your project and will be more inclined to finish the project. The angels can guide your steps and help you to stay focused. We angels know that there will be interruptions that happen, but we can help guide you back when the time is right. Think of how proud you are when you have accomplished your task!

Procrastination can also mean putting off happiness or love. Thinking you deserve love or happiness in the future can prevent you from true love and happiness now. You are worthy of love and happiness now in this present moment. You do not have to earn it. It is your divine right.

Ask for Divine guidance and help whenever you feel procrastination fears and ego-driven thoughts, keeping you from living your life to the fullest. When you co-create with your Divine team, you are unstoppable!

Love and heavenly blessings,
The Angelic Kingdom

Author Note

There are times I am very diligent and will work on a task right away, and other times, I will find ten other things to do besides what I need to do. I think procrastination is something we can all relate to at some time or another. I was guided for many years to write this book, but I did not feel qualified or worthy. I would often write several pages, and then it would be weeks before I would write again. There was school work to do as a teacher, housework, family obligations, and other distractions. I would put time restrictions on myself. I would think that I would need an hour or two to write. Then, I heard the angels tell me that I could write fifteen or twenty minutes a day and would accomplish a great deal on my book and have time for other important obligations. That time was doable, and it took the weight off my shoulders, which I had placed on myself. When I learned that procrastination was fear-based, it made so much sense to me, and I knew that I could face that fear and conquer it. When facing each challenge, I know I grow, and I become less afraid of new challenges. I am more confident and willing to try new things.

Action Steps

When faced with procrastination, follow these steps to help you accomplish your task and to feel proud of what you have done.

- Ask God and the angels to help you with the task and to take away the fears holding you back.
- List and prioritize all the projects or tasks that need to be accomplished for that day or week.
- Decide which tasks can wait and which need to be addressed.
- Break the task you have been avoiding into smaller, easier to achieve steps.
- Assign a reasonable amount of time for you to complete the task. If the task will take five hours to complete, break it up into reasonable chunks of time. Can you do one hour for five days? Can you do two and a half hours in two days?
- Compliment yourself on what you do accomplish!

Affirmation

I am able to accomplish all I need to do today. I am confident and deserving of all that God has planned for me.

Prayer

Dear God, I ask that you help me accomplish all I need to do today. I ask you to help take away any fears that keep me from my tasks. I know that working together we can accomplish great things. Amen

Journal Reflection

Take some time to reflect and journal on what projects hold you back, or you feel you are procrastinating in doing. Take some time to reflect if you think it is due to fear of failure, success, or lack of confidence in your abilities. How can you break your task down into smaller steps?

Romance

Dearest One,

Love and romance are two great gifts God has given people and desires for his children to experience. God and the angels hear many prayers and requests from people asking God to help them find true love. God also hears the prayers of those who have suffered heartache or betrayal. Falling in love and experiencing pain and heartbreak are life lessons that can teach and enable humans to grow on many levels. Each time you experience romance or a new partner, there are lessons for each of you to learn as a couple and as individuals. Romance ignites feelings of love, passion, sex, and desire. It is two people sharing their lives, hopes, and dreams with each other. It is a chance to connect on a deeper level. Romance gives partners opportunities to recognize the beauty and wonder in each other. It is a time to affirm that the person with you is lovable, attractive, and possesses gifts that are desirable to you. Romance affirms that you are lovable, attractive, and have many gifts to share.

Do you know there are Romance Angels to help you find a romantic partner and to help you communicate, love, and grow with your partner? These angels are small in stature but are mighty in love and power. The Romance Angels will whisper guidance in your ears and will guide you to the right partner for you.

The first thing Romance Angels will do is to ask you to work on loving yourself. The Romance Angels will give you loving guidance on ways you can prepare yourself for the partner you desire. They will encourage you to love yourself in emotional, physical, and spiritual ways. They know that when you love yourself, you will attract a loving partner who finds the real you, attractive and desirable. Romance Angels will ask you to surround yourself with romantic resources or activities like buying flowers for yourself, watching a romantic movie, talking to yourself in loving and self-affirming ways, and creating healthy habits.

Romance Angels, like your Guardian Angels, will whisper messages in your ears or will send their messages through people, media, or intuitive thoughts you receive. You may get messages to join a new club, try out a new coffee shop, or call an old friend. Heed these messages dear one, for you, may meet your new partner through these channels,

If you are married or in a loving partnership already, the Romance Angels can help you communicate better with your spouse or breathe new romantic sparks or interest in your current relationship.

Call on these loving beings to bring you the love and romance you deserve and desire.

Love and heavenly blessings,
The Angelic Kingdom

Author Note

We are all searching for someone to share our life with. I have often marveled at how some couple's relationships seemed to happen easily and effortlessly and have remained very happy together for many years. I have also empathized with those who have been in love, married, and then later, it ended in divorce. I have many friends who choose to be single and are very happy with their choice, and then I have friends who have waited years to be in a loving, soulmate relationship that seems to elude them for one reason or another.

The angels have taught me that we all have free will, and we make many of the choices that are before us. We may have wanted to be married but were afraid to take the next steps, and it never happened. We felt stuck in a loveless or harmful relationship but never moved out of it. We felt unworthy of true love and pushed relationships away. We may have also wanted the other person to do all the work or to rescue us. The angels also explained that although divorce is painful, many couples must go through it to break karmic ties or to break harmful patterns. Love is still present in all these situations, and our angels are with us through it all. We learn through every relationship, heartache, or joy we encounter.

The journey to find love and romance has not been an easy one for me. I had been in short term romantic relationships throughout my life and had always thought I would be married and have children. When that didn't happen for many years, I felt hurt and disappointed. I never gave up and knew that I deserved love. I knew that God would bring me the soulmate that was meant for me when the time was right for both of us. Most days, I was very happy with my life and felt very blessed. I knew what I wanted in my life and what was right for me, even if that differed from what other people thought I needed or should do to find a partner.

One day Archangel Raphael revealed to me that I needed to "get my heart back." He explained that with each relationship, we give a little or a lot of our heart to the other person. In turn, they also have given us a piece of their heart. I needed to fully get my heart back so that I could truly be myself and ready to give my heart to the person I desired. I trusted that Archangel Raphael and the angels would help me with this Spirit-driven procedure and that I would, in turn, help others to use it as well.

It was a very emotional and powerful experience. It was a time to let go of past hurts and to forgive myself and those who had hurt me. I cried for over an hour and was amazed at what had released for me. The procedure began with me sitting quietly. I asked for help and guidance. I closed my eyes and was shown the face of someone who I had a relationship with, even if it was only one date. I watched as a little angel took the piece of his heart back to him and brought my piece back to me. I said the Ho'oponopono prayer. It is a Hawaiian practice of reconciliation and forgiveness. I put my hand on my heart. I did this for each face I saw. I was not surprised by faces I had short term relationships with, but was amazed by some faces that I didn't realize would have a piece of my heart or I theirs. I was also surprised to see the faces of three women friends of mine. I had not dated them or had a romantic encounter with them. However, I was shown their faces, for they had broken my heart, my trust and our friendship. My heart hurt physically and emotionally for over a day. By the second day, I felt lighter, happier, ready for romance, and truly at peace.

Get Your Heart Back Ceremony

1. Find a comfortable place to sit and make sure you are not disturbed for at least two hours. You may want to light a candle.

2. Ask Archangel Raphael and your guardian angels to assist you.

3. Place the Ho'oponopono prayer beside you or memorize it. See the "Forgiveness" page of this book for the prayer.

4. Close your eyes and trust that God and the angels will bring you the face, name, or thought of a person you need to work with to exchange heart pieces.

5. Remember, you will probably cry, and your tears will be releasing old hurts and wounds. This method is very healing, so let the tears flow.

6. Your heart may physically and emotionally hurt for a few hours or a day.

7. You will have a sense of when the procedure is over. Thank God and the angels for this powerful ceremony. Be gentle with yourself for several hours.

Action Steps

There are many ways to bring love and romance into your life. The action steps work for individuals in a committed relationship as well as those who are single and looking to bring love and romance into their lives or wanting a soulmate relationship. The journey may take a few weeks, months, or years so be patient with yourself during the process. It will be worth the time and effort because you are worth the time and effort!

- Say I love you to yourself daily. This statement is one of the most important things we can do to bring love, romance, and abundance into our lives.
- Spend time using the "Get Your Heart Back" ceremony.
- Ask God, your Guardian Angels, and the Romance Angels to help you find the true love you deserve.
- Ask your Guardian Angels to speak with your soulmate's Guardian Angels to prepare both of you to meet and to develop a relationship.
- Begin a healthy routine.
- Wear clothes that brighten your mood.
- Get a massage or Reiki treatment.
- Do something nice for yourself every day.
- Buy flowers to brighten your home.
- Buy chocolate for yourself or someone you love.
- Watch a romantic comedy.
- Write love notes for your partner and scatter them around the house.

- Write a love note and put it in your partner's lunch bag.
- Join a cooking, art, or wellness class.
- Enroll in a club that interests you.
- Write down ten traits you would like in a romantic partner. Pray and send pink light to the list daily.
- Thank God for the soulmate he has brought into your life even before it has happened. It is trusting that God will answer your prayer.

Affirmation

I love myself, for I am lovable and worthy of love.

Prayer

Dear God, thank you for bringing great love to me. Thank you for the love and romance in my life that brings me great joy and happiness. Amen

Journal Reflection

1. What are some ways you can bring romance into your life starting today?

2. If you are looking for a partner, begin journaling on what traits you would want in a loving partner.

3. What wonderful qualities do you have that would attract a loving partner?

Signs From Heaven

Dearest One,

Many people wish to see signs or messages from God and the angels. God and we angels are happy to send you heavenly communication in the form of words, symbols, or objects. There is no limit to how many signs you may receive or how many times you call upon us. It is our heavenly mission to assist you in all ways. It brings us great joy when you ask for guidance and then heeds the guidance given. We bring God's messages to you in unlimited ways. We hear every request for help. You may call us by name or just by saying the word "Angels!" will call us to your side. Once you notice our signs, tell others what you have seen and heard. It may inspire them to call on their angels as well. We also ask that you say the words "thank you" after receiving these gifts. This gratitude benefits you and increases the blessings and gifts you will receive. Share your gifts and blessings with others so that God's loving kingdom will grow on earth.

Love and heavenly blessings,
The Angelic Kingdom

Author Note

There are many topics in this book that describe signs or messages I have received from God and the angels. I have many friends and family members who have also witnessed these lovely reminders of how close God and the angels are to us. I have had numerous occasions when I have found a feather or a penny in a strange place. I often see the number sequences of 44 or 444, which means angels are all around me. On several occasions, I have noticed cloud formations that look like angels or angel wings.

Angels may show their presence by gently stroking your hair, or you feel a warmth around you like a loving embrace. When asking for signs, you might be drawn to look at a particular sign or billboard, and the word "angel" is on it. Often, messages will come through in the lyrics of a song or on a TV show. One of the most common ways people describe receiving a message is from other people or a book. Angels will enlist people to be "earth angels" and will deliver a message through conversations, emails, or letters to others. Many people report opening a book and reading a small passage, and it is just what they needed to hear. There are many books on angels and angelic card decks that will also deliver heavenly communication for those seeking guidance and validation.

I want to share a funny story with you about a time when the angels made their presence known to me. I will warn any male readers that this story involves talking about the monthly process women go through when we experience our "period." Some women will go through their monthly cycles without many symptoms, and others will experience symptoms of fatigue, crankiness, bloating, severe cramps, cravings, and even a feeling of extreme forgetfulness of what is happening to their bodies. I am with the second group of women. One day, I was experiencing all these symptoms quite strongly. The loss of memory or forgetfulness had set in. I was wondering what was happening to me that day. I was very irritable, and the cramps made it impossible to sit or stand for very long. I had no patience for my students or colleagues, and many of my students seemed to be in trouble that day. It was one of those days when nothing seemed to be going well, so I asked for help from the angels. When the help didn't seem to come immediately, I lost patience with the angels as well. Needless to say, I was not in a good place, and I was not my usual self. It was a long day, and I did not get home until after 8:00 that evening. I was tired, hungry, in pain, and angry. It is very out of character for me to begin yelling, but that is just what I did. I yelled at God and the angels and was questioning where they were all day. Why hadn't they helped me?

Since I heard no answer and wasn't in the mood to wait patiently for an answer, I searched for supplies for my period and a large carton of ice cream. I was out of both. As you can imagine, this did not go over well with me. It was cold, and it was snowing, and now I needed to go back outside to the store. I began yelling again. I went to the store and bought what I needed. When I got home, I opened the box of panty liners. There were twenty-four little pink packets in this box. I took out a little pink package and opened it. There inside the packet was a *penny*. I fell to the ground and immediately began to cry. I felt an incredible sense of love and warmth around me. My symptoms went away, and I was at peace. That penny sits on a shelf where I keep other sacred objects. The angels had been with me all along.

Action Steps

Ask the angels for a sign that they are around you and trust that it will happen. You can be sure it is from them if you immediately think of angels when you find an object or hear something that involves angels. Once you begin to recognize signs, they will send you more.

Affirmation

I am open to receiving signs from God and the angels. I am happy to communicate with my divine team.

Prayer

Dear God, I am thankful that you are near me and for showing me your presence in my life. I am truly blessed. Amen

Journal Reflection

Journal what signs have been sent to you. How do the signs make you feel?

What signs would you like to receive? Have you asked for a sign?

Silence

Dearest One,

Silence can be a beautiful part of your day. Your world can be full of noise, and taking time for some quiet time can be uplifting and very beneficial. The silence can be a time of prayer or just a time to be still and let the cares from the day slip away. It can be a time of renewal of mind, body, and spirit. In the silence, you can hear the voice of God speaking to your heart. You can listen to the angels whispering words of love and guidance. Do not strain to hear us. Take deep breaths and relax your mind and body. We ask you to try and limit any possible distractions. Do not worry if random thoughts come your way. You can acknowledge these thoughts and then let them go.

Prayer is listening and talking to God. He hears your prayers and will answer them. It may not always be in the manner in which you think or desire, but God will answer your prayers. God knows what is best for you and will answer your prayers in ways that you cannot even imagine!

Love and heavenly blessings,
The Angelic Kingdom

Author Note

At times, we can be very limited in our thinking and what we desire. God is limitless! It is not a sign of greediness if we ask for more. When we receive, we are asked to share. When we are blessed, the blessings increase for those around us.

When I pray for something specific, I like to add the phrase, "I ask for this or something better." That way, I try not to limit my thinking and let God decide what the best answer to my prayer should be.

I listen to God and the angels in the silence. You can hear God and the angels as well. Many clients will remark that they are not able to hear the angels like I am able too. However, anyone can listen to God and the angels when they open their hearts and mind. It takes practice, but it can be done. You will probably think that you only hear your thoughts. However, God inspires your thoughts and co-creates with you. Your thoughts become new ideas and answers to your prayers. The more you take time to be silent, the more your body relaxes, and the more peaceful you will become. You will begin to feel less stressed and will feel more positive and hopeful. You will hear the messages God and the angels are bringing you each day. Ask that your ego step out of the way and then trust whatever comes to you. Tell the angels that you wish to hear them loud and clear. If possible, try to pray at the same time every day. Don't give up! They will make their presence known to you!

Action Steps

Spend time each day in silence. Spending even five minutes a day will yield benefits. Spending time with God fills you up and helps you tackle your day with love, energy, and hope.

Affirmation

I am gifted with moments of silence. I am at peace with myself and the world.

Prayer

Dear God, I know you hear my prayers. Please help me to listen to your guidance and to follow it. Amen

Journal Reflection

Journal the thoughts that come to you. Read your journal often to see what messages come through for you. Do you notice any patterns in the messages you are receiving?

Spirit Animals

Dearest One,

You may have heard of animal spirit guides. Animals have a clear, distinct line to the Divine. Your planet could not survive without the animal kingdom. Animal guides are real, and they share their wisdom with you. Many books describe animal guides and their messages.

Many animals are Power Animals to humans. You may have a strong Power Animal that is assigned to you throughout most of your life. You may have other Power Animals that come to you at various times in your life when you need their help and guidance.

Ancient cultures, as well as Native American Indian cultures, know and respect the importance of the animal kingdom and the wisdom it provides. Animals speak to us in everyday ways. Have you noticed the sounds the birds make before a storm? Have you seen the busy work of the squirrels before the cold winds of winter blow? You have heard character traits given to animals such as clever as a fox, wise as an owl, brave as a tiger, and strong as an ox, to name a few. Various cultures knew and understood the special traits each animal has and how it helps it to survive. Perhaps, you have seen a fox lately or a picture of a fox several times. The message may be that a new and clever idea is coming to you. You may notice a butterfly land near you or seems to fly around you several times this could be a message from a deceased loved one or it may indicate a time of transition for you in your life. How many times have you heard a story of a pet saving the life of its owner? There have been many stories documented about pets lying near or on a person's body part that contained cancer cells. These animals had messages for their human friends.

Animals may come to you in dreams, or you may be drawn to a particular animal, or an animal may come across your path, take

143

note and look on the Internet or in a book about what the animal represents and what it is telling you. Some spirit animals will stay with you for a long time, others just until you receive and understand their message. The animal kingdom has much to share with you. Listen and learn from their wisdom.

Love and heavenly blessings,
The Angelic Kingdom

Author Note

I have bought several books on animal messages, and I find them to be very interesting and very accurate. I have always been drawn to bears, and after reading up on bear messages, I learned that bear is a spirit guide for educators and healers. I was a first-grade teacher for over thirty-four years and began my healing practice over fifteen years ago. Bear in my life made a lot of sense. One late January morning, I went to house sit for my brother and sister-in-law. They were only a few hours out of town when a neighbor called me to inform me that a robbery had taken place in a home two houses down. Obviously, it was very upsetting and unnerving news. After I hung up the phone, I noticed several birds in the front yard. Suddenly, a blue jay flew and hit the window where I was standing. It startled me, and I was afraid the bird was hurt. The bird flew around several times and seemed to be fine. I knew that was a message for me. I looked it up on the internet. The message stated that seeing a blue jay meant safety and protection. I was so happy to receive that message!

As I took more notice of animals around me, I began to learn more about them and myself. I often would take walks around a lake in my city. I began to notice the animals that I encountered. If a particular insect, bird, or another animal, caught my attention, I knew I needed to look up the meaning of that animal and reflect on what meaning it had in my life at the time.

Action Steps

This week notice any animals or insects that seem to capture your attention. Look up spirit animals or guides on the Internet or buy a book on spirit animals. See if the animal you noticed is listed. What message does the animal have for you? The more you take notice of the animal kingdom, the more messages will come for you. Enjoy their loving wisdom and guidance for you.

Affirmation

I am guided by Spirit Animals. I am grateful for their wisdom.

Prayer

Dear God, I am thankful for the messages and guidance you give me. I am grateful for the Animal Kingdom and the wisdom they provide. Please help me to notice the signs given by you or the animals. Please help me to follow this wisdom to improve my life and the life of those around me. Amen

Journal Reflection

1. Take a walk in a park or around your neighborhood. What animals do you notice? Journal the first thoughts that come to you.

2. Has there been an animal that you have always been drawn to? Journal why you like this animal.

3. Look up the animal on a spirit animal website or buy a book on spirit animals. What does this animal say to you?

The Power of Positive Thinking

Dearest One,

We wish to impress upon you the importance and the power of positive thinking. Thoughts have form and bond together negative thoughts bond with negative thoughts and positive thoughts bond with positive thoughts. There is a universal law that states like attracts like. Simply put, positive thoughts attract more positive thoughts and negative thoughts attract more negative thoughts. If a person focuses on negative thinking, actions, or situations, the universe will respond with more of the same. Likewise, when a person strives to be kind, grateful, and positive, the universe will respond with positive people, situations, and opportunities. We would like you to picture yourself holding a huge bundle of balloons. Each balloon contains a thought. Does your bouquet of balloons hold more negative or positive thoughts? The positive balloons are light weight and colorful. The negative balloons seem to weigh you down and may appear darker in nature.

It is natural for you to have negative and positive thoughts throughout your day. We are encouraging you to notice what type of thinking occupies most of your day. We would like you to consider a typical day. Do you surround yourself with negative thinking or positive thinking people at home or work? What type of conversations do you engage in? Are you engaged in complaining or gossip behavior or conversations that encourage and support others and yourself? How do you respond to positive or negative topics? What kind of TV shows or movies do you choose to watch? Do you have any inspirational messages from artwork, calendars, quotes, videos, or books that uplift you daily?

We know that you are not able to avoid all negativity. There will be days that you feel less than favorable; however, we invite you to call on your guardian angels to help you increase positive experiences and energy around you. We will gently guide you to cancel a negative thought and replace it with a positive one. We will surround you with angelic light to keep negative energy from you. We will help you shine your beautiful light in all aspects of your life.

Love and heavenly blessings,
The Angelic Kingdom

Author Note

It takes daily practice and discipline to replace negative thoughts with purposeful, loving, positive thoughts. However, it can be done, and the universe responds in loving and abundant ways. I have worked on this for several years and have made significant progress. However, I too. can get caught up in a negative conversation or in a movie or TV show that is full of negative drama. I have made personal choices to avoid certain media that makes me feel anxious, angry, or promotes fear. Several years ago, I was hooked on a TV drama. I had watched this show for many years and had become involved in the characters and story-lines. On the show, two characters were in love and had gone through many trying times to be together. The audience was rooting for this couple, and when they finally married, the audience rejoiced! However, TV dramas need drama and tragedy to keep the story-lines going. I was devastated when the happiness ended, and new situations or characters were introduced to the show. Suddenly, one night I realized that my empathy for the characters was negatively impacting my life. When the characters were sad, I was as well. When the characters were anxious or afraid, so was I. It seemed that the characters were only happy for a short time. I stopped watching the show for several weeks and realized I was much happier. I now limit what kinds of shows I watch, and it has truly made a difference in my life.

It can be very easy to get caught up in gossip or repeat a story over and over again or to get swept away in social media topics. I am guilty myself of replaying a bad day or situation repeatedly to whoever will listen to me. The angels have taught me that replaying a negative situation over and over again keeps the energy of the situation around me, and it is harder to break through it. When I realize that I am thinking of creating a negative thought, I stop and say, "I clear, cancel, and delete that thought." Then I replace the thought with a positive one. A negative thinking example could be, "I will never find a new job! I have been looking for months!" Delete that thinking and change the words to "I have a new, exciting job that challenges me. God and the angels have guided me to this job, and I am truly grateful." Feel the energy that surrounds each example. The negative thought is heavy and filled with despair. The positive example is filled with confidence, hope, and faith, believing that God and the angels will solve the situation. If I need to interact with negative thinking people, I ask the angels to protect me and to guide me to not to add to the drama or negative conversations and not to take the negativity with me. I remind myself that it is not my drama. Remember, you are not alone, and the angels will help you to transform your thinking and your life.

Action Steps

Take some time to reflect on what positive or negative circumstances or relationships you are in right now. How can you decrease or increase the likelihood of attracting more positive situations and people into your life? Practice daily, replacing negative thoughts with positive ones. It is important to remember to say, "I will now clear, cancel, and delete" any thought that does not serve you or others.

Affirmation

I think, act, and speak in positive and loving ways.

Prayer

Dear God, please help me to speak and act in positive ways so that I can bring only good into my life. Thank you for your help. Amen

Journal Reflection

Take time to reflect and journal on what TV shows or movies that you watch. Are there any shows that make you feel anxious, nervous, or fearful? How does your body react to these shows? Do you have dreams at night with these shows in mind? What TV shows or movies make you feel good?

Are there any people around you that are positive and uplifting? What do you admire about them?

Trust our Signs

Dearest One,

Many humans do not always trust that their prayers, thoughts, and questions are answered. They do not trust that we angels are closer to them than they can ever imagine. We are with you night and day, supporting, guiding, and protecting you. Our love is unconditional. Humans do not need to earn our love. It is and always will be available for you and all humans. We speak in many ways. We speak to your heart. It is how God communicates with you. Your spirit and the Divine Spirit of God work together to give you messages and signs. Your gut feelings or intuition are real. Trust them! You have heard of the power of "woman's intuition." Know that this is true and real. However, this is not reserved only for women. It is meant for men, women, and children of all ages.

We speak to you through books. Have you ever opened a book and read exactly what you needed to read, see, or feel? This is no accident! We have guided you to find what you needed to read to answer your prayers and to let you know we are near. We also speak to you through music and lyrics to songs. You may hear the same song repeatedly, and the lyrics speak to you deeply and wonderfully. You may also hear messages from TV shows. As you watch a TV show, you might notice that a particular character is going through a situation that is similar to what you are going through. You may notice what the other characters are saying and notice how the dialogue is also speaking to you.

As angels, we may draw your attention to bulletin board notices, brochures, or posters advertising a class, a lecture, or an event that would help benefit you and answer your prayers. We also enlist humans to relay messages. Our messages come in groups of three. For instance, perhaps a friend mentions that she would like to begin a yoga class. You realize that you have also been thinking of joining a class. Then maybe a family member mentions that he has been taking yoga for over a year and is enjoying it. Finally, you get an email about yoga classes beginning in your area.

Sometimes, you may notice these signs and messages from us and wonder if it is a true message or just a coincidence. Do not worry, dear one. There are no coincidences. If you still need proof, we will send you the sign over and over again. A good rule of thumb is when you see, hear, or feel a message three times or more; it was meant for you!

Love and heavenly blessings,
The Angelic Kingdom

Author Note

There are many times I have received messages through TV, radio, road signs, or through other people. Once you begin noticing the signs and trusting them, you will receive more messages. One of my favorite stories about angelic messages, involves a sign in front of an apartment building. A few years ago, I was traveling to a city for a funeral. The city was two hours away from home. When I arrived, I realized that all the street parking was meter parking. I had assumed that the church would have a parking lot. I checked my purse. I had a one-dollar bill and some pennies. I always used my debit card and had not thought about getting more cash or change. I was hoping I could freshen up at a local gas station or convenience store before the service began. I drove around the streets by the church and could not find a gas station or convenience store anywhere. I drove around four or five times. I was getting nervous that I was going to be late for the service. I had arrived in plenty of time, but now there were only fifteen minutes before the service. Then I remembered to ask for help from the angels. Suddenly, I saw a sign out in front of an apartment building that read "Angel Reality." They had heard me! I turned left at the next block, and there was a gas station. The gentleman at the counter was very nice. He gave me quarters for the meter and a key to the restroom. I went back to the church and made it in time for the service with ten minutes to spare!

Action Steps

Ask the angels for a clear sign that they hear your requests. Trust me, they are! Sometimes, we humans need reassurance! They will send you a sign. If you don't hear it or see it, keep asking! You find a penny or a feather in an unusual place. You see a sign or a billboard on your morning commute that speaks of angels or relates to a current situation you are experiencing. You might see a notice or a pamphlet on a bulletin board. You may see the number sequence of 444 many times. The number 444 means that angels are all around you. Once you begin to notice these signs, they will send you more!

Affirmation

I am open to signs from God and the angels. I am grateful for their loving messages.

Prayer

Dear God, I ask that you hear my prayers for help and guidance. Please send me signs and messages that I can see, hear, and understand. I thank you all for this divine help. Amen

Journal Reflection

It is inspiring to find a penny or a feather in a strange place. I know the angels have placed these items in my path to let me know they are around me and are hearing my prayers. Ask for a sign or an object to be placed in your path. Journal on what the angels sent you and how you felt about this heavenly communication.

Visualization

Dearest One,

Visualization is very powerful and can increase success in all you do. Visualizing is a powerful tool that you possess. Simply close your eyes and picture in your mind what it is you wish to achieve or bring into your life. Manifesting and visualizing go hand in hand.

Picture yourself and others as happy and healthy. Picture it daily, and it will be so! Picture yourself abundantly blessed with time, money, family, and friends. Picture it daily, and it will be so! Picture yourself completing a special project or task. Picture it daily, and it will be so!

Your thoughts and visual pictures can create the story of your life. Create your pictures with positive thoughts and positive images and watch how your life evolves and changes. Ask the angels to help you with this process. They are happy to do so!

Love and heavenly blessings,
The Angelic Kingdom

Author Note

Visualization is not a new concept. There are many top executives and motivational speakers that use this technique to help their employees and clients to visualize and achieve success. I use visualization techniques weekly. I have found that the more I visualize what it is I want, the clearer I become in knowing just what I want, and the quicker it comes to me. Let me explain that last sentence. At times, we may say we want more money, or we want a relationship or a new job. We often are not clear on just what we wish God and the universe to bring us. Someone comes into your life. However, it is not the kind of person that you were desiring. Be specific! What type of relationship do you want? What kind of person are you hoping to meet? Is it a romantic relationship? Is it a friendship? What qualities are you looking for in this new relationship? Think about what you want and picture in your mind daily.

Why do you want more money? How will you use the money that comes to you? You may say that you wish you had more money in a checking or savings account. Be specific! Remember, more money could be $5.00 or $5,000. Picture in your mind how much money you desire. Picture it in a checking account or savings account or both. Think about how you will spend it. Visualize the money in your life. Do not worry about how it will come. Just believe and have faith.

A new job opportunity comes your way, but it is not what you were hoping for in your career. Be specific! What kind of job do you want? What are you doing at this new job? Daily visualize what kind of career you would like and then trust that it will happen.

I have experienced the universe bringing me an item that I wanted but not exactly what I wanted. I thought several times, that I would like a different toaster. One day, a friend asked me if I would like a toaster that she had. It was fairly new and seemed in good shape. I accepted it gratefully. However, it didn't last long, and bagels did not work very well in it. So, I became clearer about what I wanted. I wanted a new toaster that had slots big enough for two bagels. Soon, I saw a toaster for sale in a local store. It was just how I had pictured it. It was for me.

I decided that I needed a new bag for carrying many items when I travel. I knew just what kind of bag I wanted, and I knew how big I wanted it to be. I stated out loud what I wanted. I pictured it in my head several times. A few weeks later, my sister in law asked if I wanted a brand-new bag that she had received. She had two and didn't need one of them. It was exactly what I wanted and needed!

You can visualize big and small things. It works the same way for any size dreams and wishes you have. There is an old saying that states, "God helps those who help themselves." We are co-creators with God. However, just saying it doesn't always bring the desired results. I pray for what I want to bring in my life, and I picture it coming true. Each time I visualize what it is I want to bring in my life, I begin to feel the excitement of it coming true. It becomes a part of me. I have faith that God will provide it for me.

The feelings that come with your visualization is what is most important. If you feel it is just a dream and doubt that it will come true, you are probably right; it won't. If you believe it will come true and feel positive, happy thoughts with your visualization, it will come true! The more you visualize it, the more it is part of you. Often, people will ask me what if I am not doing it, right? What if my visualizations aren't the best they can be? I reply that the act of visualizing will bring results. It is taking action steps toward things you desire. I like to pray, and I add the words, "I ask for this or something better." I let God take the lead and allow him to bring what the best picture in my mind should and will be. Bring your dreams into reality!

Action Steps

Schedule some quiet time when you will not be interrupted for at least ten minutes. Think about what you wish to bring into your life. How do you see it in your mind? Is there anyone else involved in your visualization story? How do you feel? If you feel your visualization isn't quite right, you can change it! Tap into your senses. What do you see? What do you feel? Is there anything you can taste or smell? Do you hear anything? Think of your visualization as a work of art. Picture a blank canvas. Add as many details as you can. This daily exercise can bring you the life you have literally dreamed of living!

Affirmation

I am co-creating with God what I truly deserve and desire in my life.

Prayer

Dear God, there are many things I desire in my life. I ask that you help me bring people, opportunities, and abundance into my life. I also ask that you help me share these loving gifts with others. Amen

Journal Reflection

Take some time to journal and reflect on something you truly would like to come into your life. Try something small at first. For example, ask God and the angels to bring you a free cup of coffee. Watch what happens in the next few days or weeks. Did you notice the gift when it happened? Who gave you this gift?

Then ask for something else. What else do you wish to manifest in your life?

Weather

Dearest One,

Your earth and climate are tremendously affected by the weather. Weather not only affects plants and animals, but it affects your body and emotions as well. Humans are not meant to stay indoors for long periods. Humans need fresh air and sunshine to grow, prosper, and to live happier and healthier lives.

Weather can change your moods. The next time your mood changes negatively due to weather, stop and pause for a few seconds. Take time to reflect on the weather and your mood. What can a rainy day teach you? What blessings does it hold? Does a blizzard allow you to stay home and cuddle with your family? Does bad weather allow you to stop and pray to God for help and assistance? Would you appreciate the beautiful sunny days if every day was sunny? Do you not need the moisture of the rain and snow to give needed water to the trees, plants, and animals? Do you not need the rain to fill your water supply? Do you know that the wind blows in new and powerful changes?

Remember, God is with you through it all. His hand causes the weather and the seasons to change. God creates miracles every day in nature. Spend some time in nature each day. Notice how your mood changes and improves. Notice the miracles that come your way. Take time to bless the weather. Express gratitude for the rain, snow, and sunshine. Will you be a dark cloud or the sunshine in someone else's day today?

Love and heavenly blessings,
The Angelic Kingdom

Author Note

Weather is a universal topic. It is something we all talk about, yet we can't control. It is part of our daily lives. What we can do is ask God and the angels to help us through the weather changes. I have had firsthand experience in watching how the angels can help us during the weather. I have asked angels to guide me in driving in wintery or rainy weather. The help has always come. I have asked angels to stop the down pouring rain, so that I can get in my apartment with my armload of groceries. I have witnessed the rain stopping long enough for me to get into my apartment. The angels have helped me every time I have asked!

I experienced a miracle a few years ago. It was a sunny day in February. The snow had melted, and it felt almost like spring that morning! I went out to my car, and it started snowing. At first, I thought it was snow blowing from the roof of my apartment complex. Then I looked around. There were a few cars in the parking lot, but there was no snow falling on them. There was no snow falling on the trees or the nearby sidewalk. The snow was only falling on me and my car! It was a beautiful white snow and it shimmered in the sun. I knew instantly it was the angels sending me a message that they were around me! It was a lovely way to start my day!

Action Steps

When you wake up, take time to pray and ask for God and the angels to guide your day. Ask them to protect you that day from any weather. Give thanks for the weather, and look for the blessings it brings.

Affirmation

I am able to embrace the weather and the changes it brings in my life.

Prayer

Dear God, thank you for your handiwork in creating the weather and the seasons. Help keep me safe during bad weather and help me appreciate the sunny days you bring my way. Help me to see the blessings in all kinds of weather. Amen

Journal Reflection

How does the weather affect you? Do you spend enough time outdoors?

What is your favorite season? Why is it your favorite?

Journal the ways you can spend more time in nature to enhance your mood and to increase your oxygen levels.

Wisdom

Dearest One,

You are very wise because wisdom comes from God, who is the source of your being. True wisdom comes from within. Trust your intuition and guidance from God and the angels. Trust that the experiences you have and the people around you are all teaching you valuable lessons. You, in turn, are teaching others lessons as well. You may not even realize this is happening. However, the people in your life are there for specific reasons. They are there to help you grow, learn, and love. You are in their lives to teach them and to help them grow, learn, and love. If you are a parent, you know that you have taught your child or children valuable lessons. In turn, your child has taught you lessons on love, playtime, innocence, and laughter. There is something new to learn every day. Some lessons and experiences you learn and understand very quickly, and you are ready for greater knowledge. Other lessons may take days, weeks, or even years to master.

It is important to accept and acknowledge this wisdom that comes to you daily. Each day spend some quiet time talking and listening to God. Trust that your intuition is your inner connection and guide to God. Yes, it is true that knowledge and wisdom also come from books, movies, lectures, and classes. God is the source of all wisdom, who inspires the authors, teachers, preachers, and filmmakers to create books, classes, lectures, movies, and sermons.

A sage person listens to their inner guidance and acquires knowledge from other sources and applies it to their lives each day. Live in the present moment and trust that each moment is a step, guided by God, on your journey.

Love and heavenly blessings,
The Angelic Kingdom

Author Note

I have been a teacher for most of my life. I loved spending time with little ones and teaching them how to add and subtract, how to read and write, and how to talk to God. We are all teachers and learners in many ways. School is just one way we learn. Wisdom comes from many places and many people. We learn from our teachers, parents, friends, coworkers, and children in our life. Our greatest lessons may come from people that we have the hardest time being around. True wisdom means that we are willing to learn and grow each day. It is a lifelong journey. Stop and think about the people in your life. What are they teaching you? What are you teaching them? Have you stopped learning? What inspires you to learn more?

Action Steps

What are you interested in learning more about? What is pulling at your heart or mind to develop or learn? There are many ways to learn, and many ways to teach. Find something new this week and dedicate time to learn more about it.

Ideas:

- Join an art class at the local community center.
- Visit an art or history museum.
- Go online and learn more about a topic that interests you.
- Find and attend a lecture at a local college or university.
- Join a bible study group.
- Watch a game show that challenges your thinking and learning.
- Download a word or puzzle game app that challenges you.
- Volunteer your time to teach others a skill that you enjoy.
- Buy a crossword or word search puzzle book.

- Read a new book.
- Enroll in a class that interests you or will further your career.

Affirmation

I am a teacher and a student. I am growing in wisdom and love each day.

Prayer

Dear God, you are the source of all wisdom and understanding. I ask you to guide me to keep learning and growing. Send your angels to show me an area I can grow. Thank you for your love, help, and guidance. Amen

Journal Reflection

1. What is something you have always wanted to do or learn more about? What tugs at your heart just waiting for you to try? Spend some time reflecting and journaling on these questions.

2. Spend some time researching ways to learn more about the topics or speakers that inspire you.

Worrying

Dearest One,

We know that your life is busy and full of many things to think about and do. We would like you to limit or stop filling your mind and life with worry. Worrying is a waste of time. Worrying does nothing but bring disharmony to the mind and body. Some humans will even go as far as to say that needless worrying, creates lines on their faces. Worry and guilt are lower energies that have adverse effects. Prayer, meditation, and talking to God and the angels have only positive and peaceful effects.

Although we know that all humans worry from time to time, we ask that you not stay in this state of mind for very long. Your real state of being is peace. Give your cares and worries to God. God can dispel your fears and worries and bring you back to your true peaceful self. Ask the angels to take your fears and worries and lay them at the feet of God. Does God need to worry? You are a child of God. So then, why worry?

Love and heavenly blessings,
The Angelic Kingdom

Author Note

Letting go of our control and letting God take over is not always easy to do. It is trusting that God is in charge and knows what is best for us. Since I began talking to angels, I now worry less. I pray to God for help and ask the angels to take my prayers and worries to God. I ask that God's will and not mine happen. God has a better plan than I could ever create. If I believe in God's perfect order, then why should I worry? However, we are human. We worry. We get scared. It takes practice to let God take over. Yet, it can be done.

When a situation comes up that worries me, I talk to God about it. Then I ask the angels to please put out their hands. I place my fears and worries in their hands. I ask them to take these worries and place them before God. This brings me a feeling of peace and comfort. I find that my worry turns to peace. My worry turns to trust. My trust turns into a life filled with peace. My worries disappear, and joyful solutions appear. I am filled with gratitude.

Action Steps

When you are worried about a situation, pray, and talk to God about your worries. Then close your eyes and picture an angel standing in front of you. Place your worries in their hands. Visualize the angel flying off with your concerns and placing them in front of God. If you still feel worried and cannot seem to let go, repeat this exercise until you feel you are letting go. Notice what happens to your emotions and your body as you let go. When the situation is resolved, give thanks and gratitude to God and the angels. Remember, this may take practice. The more you let go, the easier it is to let God take control.

Affirmation

I trust God to take my worries. I am at peace.

Prayer

Dear God, please help me to worry less and trust more. Help me to feel peace and reassurance that you will always provide for my loved ones and me. You know what I need before I even ask. Help me to also receive your peace and gifts with an open and grateful heart. Thank you for your love, help, and guidance. Amen

Journal Reflection

Journal what is causing your worry or anxiety? What can you give to God? After a week or two, journal how you feel after giving your worries to God.